我的演讲美文
神奇的时代

英汉对照　词汇解析　语法讲解　励志语录

李　琦　编著

中国纺织出版社

图书在版编目（CIP）数据

我的演讲美文：神奇的时代：英文/李琦编著. -- 北京：中国纺织出版社，2019.4
ISBN 978-7-5180-5096-3

Ⅰ.①我… Ⅱ.①李… Ⅲ.①英语—语言读物②演讲—世界—选集 Ⅳ.① H319.4：I

中国版本图书馆 CIP 数据核字（2018）第 119972 号

责任编辑：武洋洋　　责任印制：储志伟

中国纺织出版社出版发行
地址：北京市朝阳区百子湾东里A407号楼　邮政编码：100124
销售电话：010—67004422　传真：010—87155801
http://www.c-textilep.com
E-mail:faxing@c-textilep.com
中国纺织出版社天猫旗舰店
官方微博http://www.weibo.com/2119887771
三河市延风印装有限公司印刷　各地新华书店经销
2019年4月第1版第1次印刷
开本：880×1230　1/32　印张：6
字数：200千字　定价：39.80元

凡购本书，如有缺页、倒页、脱页，由本社图书营销中心调换

前言

　　思想结晶改变人生命运，经典美文提高生活品位。曾几何时，一个字，触动你的心弦；一句话，让你泪流满面；一篇短文，让你重拾信心，勇敢面对生活给你的考验。这就是语言的魅力。通过阅读优美的英文短文，不仅能够扩大词汇量，掌握单词的用法，了解语法，学习地道的表达，更让你的心灵如沐春风，得到爱的呵护和情感的滋养。

　　岁月流转，经典永存。针对英语学习爱好者的需要，编者精心选取了难易适中的英语经典美文，为你提供一场丰富多彩的文学盛宴。本书采用中英文对照的形式，便于读者理解。每篇美文后都附有单词解析、语法知识点、经典名句三大版块，让你在欣赏完一篇美文后，还能扩充词汇量、巩固语法知识、斟酌文中好句，并感悟人生。在一篇篇不同题材风格的英语美文中，你总能找到引起你心灵共鸣的一篇。

　　读一本新书恰似坠入爱河，是场冒险。你得全身心地投入进去。翻开书页之时，从前言直至封底你或许都知之甚少。但谁又不是呢？字里行间的只言片语不总是正确的。

　　有时候你会发现，人们自我推销时是一种形象，等你在深入了解后，他们就完全变样了。有时故事的叙述流于表面，朴实的语言，平淡的情节，但阅读过半后，你却发觉这本书真是出乎意料的妙不可言，而这种感受只能靠自己去感悟！

阅读之乐，腹有诗书气自华；阅读之美，活水云影共天光。阅读可以放逐百年孤独，阅读可以触摸千年月光。阅读中有眼前的收获，阅读中也有诗和远方。

让我们静下心来感受英语美文的温度，在英语美文中仔细品味似曾相识的细腻情感，感悟生命和人性的力量。

编者
2018年6月

目录

01 Our Family Creed
家族的信条···001

02 We Beat the Reaper by Living Fully A
我们通过充实地生活来战胜死亡 A···006

03 We Beat the Reaper by Living Fully B
我们通过充实地生活来战胜死亡 B···011

04 Teach Teachers How to Create Magic A
老师如何创造魔力 A···015

05 Teach Teachers How to Create Magic B
老师如何创造魔力 B···020

06 Teach Teachers How to Create Magic C
老师如何创造魔力 C···025

07 Change with the World and Remake America A
与时俱进，重塑美国 A··029

08 Change with the World and Remake America B
与时俱进，重塑美国 B··034

09 Change with the World and Remake America C
与时俱进，重塑美国 C··040

10 Change with the World and Remake America D
与时俱进，重塑美国 D··045

11 Change with the World and Remake America E
与时俱进，重塑美国 E··050

12 Change with the World and Remake America F
与时俱进，重塑美国 F··055

13 Heal the Children, Heal the World A
   拯救儿童，拯救世界 A·· 060

14 Heal the Children, Heal the World B
   拯救儿童，拯救世界 B·· 066

15 Mo Yan's Nobel Prize Speech A
   莫言诺贝尔文学奖演讲 A·· 071

16 Mo Yan's Nobel Prize Speech B
   莫言诺贝尔文学奖演讲 B·· 076

17 Fight for Peace A
   为和平而战 A··· 080

18 Fight for Peace B
   为和平而战 B··· 085

19 Save Our Planet A
   拯救我们的地球 A··· 089

20 Save Our Planet B
   拯救我们的地球 B··· 094

21 To Build an Effective Multilateral System A
   建立有效的多边关系 A·· 099

22 To Build an Effective Multilateral System B
   建立有效的多边关系 B·· 104

23 Stay Hungry, Stay Foolish A
   求知若饥，虚心若愚 A·· 109

24 Stay Hungry, Stay Foolish B
   求知若饥，虚心若愚 B·· 114

25 Stay Hungry, Stay Foolish C
   求知若饥，虚心若愚 C·· 119

26 Stay Hungry, Stay Foolish D
   求知若饥，虚心若愚 D·· 124

27 Stay Hungry, Stay Foolish E
   求知若饥，虚心若愚 E·· 129

Contents
目录

28 Stay Hungry, Stay Foolish F
   求知若饥，虚心若愚 F ·· 134

29 Never Selling Your Soul A
   不要出卖自己的灵魂 A ·· 139

30 Never Selling Your Soul B
   不要出卖自己的灵魂 B ·· 144

31 Never Selling Your Soul C
   不要出卖自己的灵魂 C ·· 148

32 Never Selling Your Soul D
   不要出卖自己的灵魂 D ·· 153

33 Amazing Time A
   神奇的时代 A ·· 157

34 Amazing Time B
   神奇的时代 B ·· 162

35 Focus Plus Time Equals Success A
   直觉+时间=成功 A ·· 168

36 Focus Plus Time Equals Success B
   直觉+时间=成功 B ·· 174

37 Focus Plus Time Equals Success C
   直觉+时间=成功 C ·· 178

01 Our Family Creed
家族的信条

John Davison Rockefeller, financier, oil magnate and philanthropist
约翰·戴维森·洛克菲勒的励志演讲

They are the **principles** on which my wife and I have tried to bring up our family. They are the principles in which my father believed and by which he governed his life.

They are the principles, many of them, which I learned at my mother's knee. They point the way to usefulness and happiness in life, to **courage** and peace in death.

If they mean to you what they mean to me, they may perhaps be helpful also to our sons for their guidance and **inspiration**. Let me state them: I believe in the supreme worth of the individual and in his right to life, **liberty** and the pursuit of happiness.

I believe that every right implies a responsibility; every opportunity, an **obligation**; every possession, a duty.

I believe that the law was made for man and not man for the law; that

这些都是我和我的太太在教育我们子女时尽力遵守的原则。其中一些原则是我的父辈深信不疑的为人处世的原则。

还有一些是我在我母亲膝下所学到的原则。这些信条教会我做一个有用的人，教会我快乐以及直面死亡的勇敢和安详。

假如这些信条对各位也有同我一样的意义的话，那么它们或许也有助于我们的后世子孙从中获得引导和启发。我来分享这些信条吧：我相信个人的价值至高无上，每个人都有生存的权利、自由的权利和追求幸福的权利。我相信每一项权利都意味着一种责任，每一次机遇都意味着一项义务，每一种拥有都意味着一种职责。

我相信法律是为人而量身定做的，但人却不是为法律而

government is the servant of the people and not their master.

I believe in the dignity of labor, whether with head or hand; That the world owes no man a living but that it owes every man an opportunity to make a living.

I believe that thrift is essential to well-ordered living and that economy is a prime requisite of a sound financial structure, whether in government business or personal affairs.

I believe that truth and justice are **fundamental** to an enduring social order.

I believe in the sacredness of a promise. That a man's word should be as good as his bond, that character-not wealth or power or position-is of **supreme** worth.

I believe that the rendering of useful service is the common duty of mankind and that only in the purifying fire of sacrifice is the dross of selfishness consumed and the greatness of the human soul set free.

I believe in an all-wise and all-loving God, named by whatever name, and that the individual's highest **fulfillment**, greatest happiness and widest usefulness are to be found in living in harmony with His will.

I believe that love is the greatest thing in the world; that it alone can overcome hate; that right can and will

造就的；我相信政府是人民的奴仆，而非人民的主人。

我相信无论脑力劳动还是体力劳动都是值得人们尊敬的；天下没有白吃的午餐，但它却会给每个人一次谋生的机会。

我相信勤俭是井然有序生活必需的，而节俭是健全的金融机制之根本，无论政府、商业或个人事务皆应如此。

我相信真理和公正对社会的长治久安至关重要。

我相信神圣的盟约。一个人应当言而有信，品格——无关财富、权势或者地位——应同样具有至高无上的价值。

我相信提供有用的服务是人类的共同职责，只有在炼火中献身，那些自私的渣滓才能被消除，而人类高尚的灵魂才能发挥出来。

我相信全能全知、满有爱心的上帝——不管如何称呼；个人最大的成就、最大的幸福、最大的作为，都必须依照上帝的意志才能在和谐的生活中找到。

我相信爱是世界上最伟大的事物；唯有爱才能克服仇恨；我相信公理能够而且必将战胜强权。

不管如何表达，以上就是

triumph over might.

These are the principles, however formulated, for which all good men and women throughout the world, irrespective of race or creed, education, social position or occupation, are standing, and for which many of them are suffering and dying.

These are the principles upon which alone a new world recognizing the brotherhood of man and the fatherhood of God can be established.

全世界一切善良的人们所信奉的原则，不论其种族、信仰、教育、地位或职业如何，而为了这些原则，许多人正在饱受煎熬，甚至献出生命。

唯有在这些信条的基础上，才能建立起人人亲如兄弟，上帝亲如父辈的新世界。

单词解析 Word Analysis

principle ['prɪnsəpl] *n.* 原则；原理
例 These machines work on the same principle.
这些机器按照相同的原理运转。

courage ['kʌrɪdʒ] *n.* 勇气
例 They don't have the courage to apologize for their actions.
他们没有勇气为自己的行为道歉。

inspiration [ˌɪnspə'reɪʃn] *n.* 灵感；鼓舞；启示
例 He went to church for inspiration.
他去教堂做礼拜寻找灵感。

liberty ['lɪbəti] *n.* 自由
例 We went to see the Statue of Liberty.
我们去看了自由女神像。

obligation [ˌɒblɪ'geɪʃ(ə)n] *n.* 义务；职责
例 We all have the obligation to stop the criminal act.
我们都有义务制止犯罪行为。

fundamental [fʌndə'ment(ə)l] *adj.* 基本的；根本的

例 You have to tackle the fundamental cause of the problem.
你应该处理问题最基本的原因。

supreme [suː'priːm] *adj.* 最高的；至高的

例 For me, dieting requires a supreme effort.
对于我来说，减肥需要极大的努力。

fulfillment [fʊl'fɪlmənt] *n.* 履行；实行；满足感

例 How can we attain fulfillment in this world?
我们怎样才能在这个世界上获得满足？

语法知识点 Grammar Points

① **If they mean to you what they mean to me, they may perhaps be helpful also to our sons for their guidance and inspiration.**

这个句子中有一个结构"be helpful to"，表示"对……有用；有助于"，同义词组还有be advantageous to...。

例 It is always helpful to discuss your problems with your friends.
和朋友讨论问题总是对你有帮助的。

② **I believe in the supreme worth of the individual.**

这个句子中有一个结构"believe in"，表示"信任；信仰"。注意区分believe in和believe的用法：believe in多表示信仰，多搭配宗教、理论、可信任之人；believe则多表示相信某人说的话。

例 We don't believe in ghosts.
我们不相信鬼神。

③ **I believe that thrift is essential to well-ordered living...**

这个句子中有一个结构"be essential to"，表示"对……必不可少"，同义词组有be indispensable to...。

例 Hard work is essential to success.
努力工作对成功至关重要。

Our Family Creed 家族的信条

④ **I believe in an all-wise and all-loving God, named by whatever name, and that the individual's highest fulfillment, greatest happiness and widest usefulness are to be found in living in harmony with His will.**

这个句子中有一个结构"in harmony with",表示"与……协调;与……一致"。

例 We must ensure the tourism develops in harmony with the environment.
我们必须确保旅游的发展同环境相协调。

⑤ **These are the principles, however formulated, for which all good men and women throughout the world, irrespective of race or creed, education...**

这个句子中有一个结构"irrespective of",表示"不管;不顾"。同义词组有regardless of。

例 The field gives high yields irrespective of weather.
不论天气如何,这块地总是很高产。

经典名句 Famous Classics

1. Where there is no struggle, there is no strength. — Oprah Winfrey
没有奋斗,就没有力量。(奥普拉·温弗瑞)

2. No matter how far you may fly, never forget where you come from.
无论你能飞多远,都别忘了你来自何方。

3. Growing in wisdom can be measured by the decrease in bitterness.
智慧的增长可用痛苦的减少来衡量。

4. Don't tell lies because those who believe your lies are the ones who believe in you.
不要去骗人,因为你能骗到的,都是相信你的人。

5. Never interrupt your enemy when he is making a mistake. — Napoleon Bonaparte
当你的敌人犯错的时候,千万不要去打断他。(拿破仑·波拿巴)

02 We Beat the Reaper by Living Fully A
我们通过充实地生活来战胜死亡 A

Randy Pausch, Carnegie Mellon Professor Carnegie Mellon University, September 18, 2007
兰迪·波许在卡内基·梅隆大学的演讲

I am glad to be here today. Hell, I am glad to be anywhere today.

President Cohon asked me to come and give the charge to the **graduates**. I assure you, it's nothing compared to the charge you have just given me.

This is an **incredible** place. I have seen it through so many lenses. I saw it when I was a graduate student that didn't get **admitted** and then somebody invited me back and said, OK, we'll change our mind.

And I saw it as a place that hired me back to be on the **faculty** many years later and gave me the chance to do what anybody wants to do, which is "follow their passion, follow their heart and do the things they're excited about".

And the great thing about this university unlike almost all the other ones I know of is that nobody gets in your way when you try to do it. And that's just

今天我很高兴能够来到这里。天哪，今天我不论到哪里都让我高兴。

柯汉校长要求我来到这里，给我们的毕业生带来一些鼓励。但是我向你保证，你们给我的鼓励反而更多。

这里真是个难以置信的地方。我对它有多方面的了解。因为我也是从这里毕业的，遗憾的是当时我并没有成功申请上研究生，之后他们又通过我的申请，并说，我们改主意了，你被录取了。

如我所见，多年之后我留校任教。这是一份很多人梦寐以求的教职工作，在这里你可以跟随你的热情，听从心的召唤，并能够做自己认为刺激的事情。

这里最棒的，胜过其他学校的一件事就是，当你想要实现梦想的时候，没有人会成为

We Beat the Reaper by Living Fully A
我们通过充实地生活来战胜死亡 A

fantastic.

And to the degree that a human being can love an institution. I love this place and I love all of the people and I am very grateful to Jerry Cohon and everyone else for all the kindness they have shown me.

Last August I was told that in all likelihood I had three to six months left to live. I am on month nine now and I am gonna get down and do any push-ups...But there will be a short pick-up basketball game later.

Somebody said to me, in light of those numbers, wow, so you are really beating the Grim Reaper. And what I said without even thinking about is that we don't beat the Reaper by living longer. We beat the Reaper by living well, and living fully.

For the Reaper will come for all of us, the question is what do we do between the time we are born and the time he shows up.

Because he shows up it is too late to do all the things that you're always gonna kind of "get round to". So I think the only advice I can give you on how to live your life well is, first off, remember, it's a cliche, but love cliche, "it is not the things we do in life that we regret on our death bed, it is the things we do not".

你的绊脚石。这简直太棒了!

只要是有感情的人都会爱上的地方。我爱这里,更爱这里的每一个人。我十分感谢柯汉校长和每一位同事,感谢他们对我的好意,这让我感到温暖。

去年8月,我被告知只有3~6个月可活了。现在已经是第9个月了。我准备做俯卧撑了……但是一会儿将会有一小段篮球赛。

当我说完这一串数字之后,有人跟我说,天哪,你真的战胜了冷酷的死神呀。而我则毫不犹豫地回答,仅靠多活几天是无法战胜它的,只有活得精彩、活得充实才能真正地打败它。

对于死神来说,最终它都会得到我们的生命。这从我们出生时就知道,关键是死神来拿走我们的生命前的这个过程中你都做了什么。

当死神来时,才想到做那些我们一直想做而未做之事,就已经为时晚矣。如何才能活得更好,我只能给你一条建议,那就是不要等待,马上就去做。这一点要记牢,虽然是陈词滥调。但是我爱这种陈词滥调,"我们将死之时,后悔的不是那些做过的事,而是那些没有做过的事"。

Because I **assure** you I've done a lot of stupid things and none of them bother me. All the mistakes, all the **dopey** things and all the times I was **embarrassed** they don't matter. What matter is that, I can kind of look back and say, "pretty much anytime I got a chance to do something cool, I tried to grab for it." And that's where my **solace** comes from.

坦白说,曾经犯过的所有错误,做过的蠢事和那些令我感到尴尬的时刻,现在变得都不那么重要了。真正重要的是,每当我回忆往昔,我会说:"只要有机会,能做一些很酷的事时,我就毫不犹豫去争取。"这才令我感到欣慰。做过很多愚蠢的事情,但它们没有一件烦扰着我。

单词解析 Word Analysis

graduate ['grædʒueɪt] *n.* 毕业生 *v.* 毕业

例 I would apply for that job if I were a graduate.
如果我是个毕业生的话,我会申请那个工作。

incredible [ɪn'krɛdəbl] *adj.* 难以置信的

例 It seemed incredible that people would still want to play football during a war.
人们在战争期间仍然想要踢足球这件事令人难以置信。

admit [əd'mɪt] *v.* 准许进入;承认

例 They didn't admit they were defeated.
他们不承认被打败了。

faculty ['fækəlti] *n.* 全体教员

例 He spoke on behalf of all the members of the faculty.
他代表所有教职员工讲话。

assure [ə'ʃʊr] *v.* 保证;担保

例 I assure I will be there.
我向你保证我会去那。

We Beat the Reaper by Living Fully A
我们通过充实地生活来战胜死亡 A

dopey ['dəʊpɪ] *adj.* 迟钝的；呆笨的

例 He is very nice, but a little dopey.
他人非常好，就是有点傻。

embarrassed [ɪm'bærəst] *adj.* 尴尬的

例 I was embarrassed to admit I was wrong.
我非常尴尬地承认我错了。

solace ['sɒlɪs] *n.* 安慰；慰藉

例 Music was a great solace to me when I was upset.
当我不安的时候，音乐给了我安慰。

语法知识点 *Grammar Points*

① **It's nothing compared to the charge you have just given me.**

这个句子中有一个结构"compare to"，表示"把……比作；比喻为"。要学会区分它与compare with，表示和……相比较。

例 Children are often compared to happy birds.
儿童经常被比作快乐的小鸟。
Let's compare this photo with that one.
让我们把这张照片和那张做一下比较。

② **And the great thing about this university unlike almost all the other ones I know of is that nobody gets in your way when you try to do it. And that's just fantastic.**

这个句子里有一个结构"get in one's way"，表示"挡某人的路；妨碍人"。

例 Her social life got in her way of study.
她的社交活动妨碍了学业。

③ **I love this place and I love all of the people and I am very grateful to Jerry Cohon and everyone else for all the kindness they have shown me.**

这个句子里有一个结构"be grateful to"，表示"对……感激"，相同的词组有show gratitude to和be thankful to。

例 We should always be grateful to our parents.

我们应该经常对父母感恩。

④ **Because he shows up it is too late to do all the things that you're always gonna kind of "get round to".**

这个句子里有一个结构"too...to..."，表示"太……而不能……"。

例 This dress is too expensive for her to buy.
这条连衣裙太贵了，她买不起。

经典名句 Famous Classics

1. Don't set your goals according to what are deemed important by others. Only you know what is best for yourself.
   别人认为重要的，并不就是你的追求。只有自己才知道什么最合适。

2. Nobody can go back and start a new beginning, but anyone can start today and make a new ending.
   没人能回头重新来过，但谁都可以从现在起书写一个不同的结局。

3. Every drop you drink makes your life tastier!
   点点滴滴，生活更美！

4. A good plan today is better than a perfect plan tomorrow. —*Wag the Dog*
   今天的好计划胜过明天的完美计划。（《摇尾狗》）

5. We are what we repeatedly do. Excellence, then, is not an act, but a habit.
   重复的行为造就了我们；因此，卓越不是一种举动，而是一种习惯。

读书笔记

03 We Beat the Reaper by Living Fully B
我们通过充实地生活来战胜死亡 B

Randy Pausch, Carnegie Mellon Professor Carnegie Mellon University, September 18, 2007
兰迪·波许在卡内基·梅隆大学的演讲

The second thing I would add to that, and I didn't **coordinate** on the subject of this word but I think it's the right word that comes up, is passion. And you will need to find your **passion**. Many of you have already done it, many of you will later, many of you will take till your 30s or 40s. But don't give up on finding it. Alright? Because then all you're doing is waiting for the Reaper. Find you passion and follow it.

And if there's anything I have learned in my life, you will not find passion in things. And you will not find that passion in money. Because the more things and the more money you have, the more you will just look around and use that as the **metric**, and there will always be someone with more.

So your passion must come from the things that fuel you from the inside. And honors and awards are nice things

第二件事我想补充说的是，我并没有使用"计划"这个字眼，我认为另一个字眼更合适，就是"热情"这个词。你们必须找到自己激情所在。或许你们很多人都已经有了，很多人以后总会有的，还有甚者是自己三四十岁才找到。但是千万不要放弃寻找好吗？如果你放弃了，死神就会来到你的身边了。

如果说我一生中还学到了什么的话，那就是你无法从物质上找到什么激情。更不会从金钱上找到激情。因为你拥有越多财富和金钱，你就越想去比较周围的世界，而你总是能看到比你更富有的人。

因此，你的热情必须来自于能够从内在激发你的事情。荣誉和奖励是很好的，但是这些要出于同行们对你真正的尊敬。或

but only to be the extent that they **regard** the real respect from your peers. And to be thought well of by other people that you think even more highly of is a **tremendous** honor that I've been granted.

Find you passion and in my experience, no matter what you do at work or what you do in official settings, that passion would be **grounded** in people. And it will be grounded in the relationships you have with people and what they think of you when you time comes. And if you can gain the respect of those around you, and the passion and true love, and I've said this before, but I waited till 39 to get married because I had to wait that long to find someone where her happiness was more important than mine. And if nothing else I hope that all of you can find that kind of passion and that kind of love in your life.

Thank you!

者像我一样能够得到我尊敬人的认同，这才是最大荣誉。

去寻找你的热情吧，在我看来，无论你从事何种工作或者处在怎样的工作环境之中，你的激情来自于你周围的人。激情基于人际关系，基于你离开人世时，人们对你的评价。如果你还能够赢得身边人的尊敬的话，正如我之前的热情和真爱。我直到39岁才结婚，因为我等了很久才遇到一位让我感到她的幸福比我的更重要的人。抛开这一切不谈，我愿在座的各位，此生都能够找到这样的热情和真爱。

谢谢！

单词解析 Word Analysis

coordinate [kəʊˈɔːdɪneɪt] *v.* 调整；协调

例 You must coordinate the movements of your arms and legs when swimming.
游泳时你必须使手臂和腿的动作相协调。

passion [ˈpæʃən] *n.* 激情；热情

例 His passion for the computer games has cooled down.
他对电脑游戏的热情已经冷却了。

We Beat the Reaper by Living Fully B
我们通过充实地生活来战胜死亡 B

metric ['mɛtrɪk] *adj.* 公制的；公尺的 *n.* 度量标准
例 Whatever your metric of success is, you should be positive towards what you have achieved.
不论你衡量成功的标准是什么，都应该积极地面对自己的成就。

regard [rɪ'gɑːd] *v.* 尊敬；注重；考虑
例 One must show proper regard for the teachers.
我们应该足够尊重老师。

tremendous [trɪ'mendəs] *adj.* 巨大的
例 Tremendous changes have taken place here.
这里发生了巨大的变化。

ground [graʊnd] *v.* 打基础 *n.* 地面
例 Fiction should be grounded in reality.
小说应来源于现实生活。

语法知识点 Grammar Points

① **The second thing I would add to that, and I didn't coordinate on the subject of this word but I think it's the right word that comes up, is passion.**

这个句子中有一个结构"come up"，在这里表示"被提出"。Come up 这个词还表示"走近；发生；开始；上升；发芽"。
例 The questions of wage increase came up at the meeting.
增加工资问题已经在会议中提出。
I will tell you immediately if anything comes up.
如果发生了什么事情，我将立即告诉你。

② **But don't give up on finding it.**

这个句子中有一个结构"give up on doing"，表示"放弃做某事"。和 give up doing 意思相同。give up doing 更为正式。

③ **Because the more things and the more money you have, the more you will just look around and use that as the metric, and there will always be someone with more.**

013

这个句子中有一个结构"the more..., the more...",表示"越……,越……",是比较级的用法。

例 The more you learn, the more you wish to learn.
你学的越多,就越想学。

经典名句 Famous Classics

1. There is no elevator to success. You have to take the stairs.
   成功没有电梯,只有一步一个脚印的楼梯。

2. What we know or what we believe is, in the end, of little consequence. The only consequence is what we do.
   我们知道的或相信的,本质上并不重要。唯一重要的是:我们做的。

3. Strength alone knows conflict, weakness is below even defeat, and is born vanquished.
   强者才懂得斗争;弱者没有失败的资格,而是生来就是被征服的。

4. Great things are not done by impulse, but by a series of small things brought together.
   伟大的成就并非源自一时冲动,而是由一系列小事汇聚而成的。

5. Always be a first-rate version of yourself, instead of a second-rate version of somebody else.
   永远都要做最好的自己,而不是第二好的别人。

04 Teach Teachers How to Create Magic A
老师如何创造魔力 A

Christopher Emdin, science TED, October, 2013
克里斯托弗·艾姆丁在 TED 的演讲

Right now there is an **aspiring** teacher who is working on a 60-page paper based on some age-old education theory developed by some dead education professor wondering to herself what this task that she's engaging in has to do with what she wants to do with her life, which is to be an educator, change lives, and **spark** magic. Right now there is an aspiring teacher in a graduate school of education who is watching a professor **babble** on and on about engagement in the most disengaging way possible.

Right now there's a first-year teacher at home who is pouring through lesson plans trying to make sense of standards, who is trying to make sense of how to grade students **appropriately**, while at the same time saying to herself over and over again, "Don't smile till November," because that's what she was taught in her teacher education program. Right

现在有一位有追求的老师正准备写一篇60页的论文,论文是关于源于一些古老的教育理念,而这些理念都是由一些早已逝去的教育家们研究的,于是这位老师就问自己,她正在完成的这项任务——成为一个教育者,改变生命,启迪人生——是否和她的工作有联系呢。还有一位有理想的老师,就读教育研究生院,在那里听了一位教授以一种最无聊的方式不停地重复着教育中的互动性。

现在更有一位教一年级的老师,在家中对课程计划进行复查,她试图找到达标的感觉。这位老师还在想如何才能更加合理地为学生打分,同时又反复地对自己说:"在11月前都不要微笑。"因为这些都是她从教育课程中学到的知识。有位学生正试图想出一个好主意,说服他的父母他很不舒

now there's a student who is coming up with a way to **convince** his mom or dad that he's very, very sick and can't make it to school tomorrow.

On the other hand, right now there are amazing educators that are sharing information, information that is shared in such a beautiful way that the students are sitting at the edge of their seats just waiting for a bead of sweat to drop off the face of this person so they can soak up all that knowledge. Right now there is also a person who has an entire audience **rapt** with attention, a person that is weaving a powerful narrative about a world that the people who are listening have never imagined or seen before, but if they close their eyes tightly enough, they can **envision** that world because the storytelling is so **compelling.** Right now there's a person who can tell an audience to put their hands up in the air and they will stay there till he says, "Put them down." Right now.

So people will then say, "Well, Chris, you describe the guy who is going through some awful training but you're also describing these powerful educators. If you're thinking about the world of education or urban education in particular, these guys will probably cancel each other out, and then we'll be okay."

服，所以明天不能上学了。

另一方面，一些了不起的教育家们在传授知识，以一种最优美的方式传授着，学生靠近老师的身边，只为了等待一滴甘露从老师的脸上掉下来，并从中汲取所有的知识。又有一位让所有观众全神贯注的人，他利用生动的语言，描绘着一个闻所未闻的世界，那个故事实在是太精彩了，只要你闭上眼睛就能想象出那个世界。还有一个人，他让观众们将双手伸向空中，直到他说放下，才可以放下。现在就这样吧。

人们会说，"克里斯，你在描述一个正在接受可怕训练的家伙，你也描述了那些有感召力的教育者。如果你想谈教育，或者是关注城市教育的话，那些人可能会有相反的效果并会相互抵消，我们就没事了。"

单词解析 *Word Analysis*

aspiring [ə'spaɪərɪŋ] *adj.* 有抱负的；有追求的
例 Mark Twain was an aspiring writer.
马克·吐温是个有抱负的作家。

spark [spɑːk] *v.* 发动；鼓舞 *n.* 火花；闪光
例 This proposal will spark another debate.
这个提议会引起另一个讨论。

babble ['bæb(ə)l] *v.* 喋喋不休
例 She always babbles about trifles.
她总是唠叨些琐事。

appropriately [ə'prəʊprɪətli] *adv.* 适当地；合适地
例 Try to dress appropriately when you are interviewed.
面试的时候要穿着恰当。

convince [kən'vɪns] *v.* 说服；使确信
例 He convinced me to wash the dishes.
他说服我刷了碗。

rapt [ræpt] *adj.* 全神贯注的
例 She fixed a rapt eye on him.
她全神贯注地望着他。

envision [ɪn'vɪʒn] *v.* 想象；预想
例 Try to envision a bright future.
试着展望一下美好的未来。

compelling [kəm'pelɪŋ] *adj.* 引人注目的；强制的
例 This is quite a compelling idea.
这是个非常引人注目的想法。

我的演讲美文：神奇的时代

语法知识点 *Grammar Points*

① Right now there is an aspiring teacher who is working on a 60-page paper based on some age-old education theory...

这个句子中有一个结构"based on"，做后置定语修饰paper，表示"根据；基于"。

例 The whole plan is based on his own supposition.
整个计划建立在他的臆想上。

② ...some dead education professor wondering to herself what this task that she's engaging in has to do with what she wants to do with her life, which is to be an educator, change lives, and spark magic.

这个句子中有一个结构"engage in"，表示"从事于；参加"。

例 Mr. Smith engaged in political affairs when he was in thirties.
史密斯先生在三十岁的时候从事政治事务。

③ Right now there's a first-year teacher at home who is pouring through lesson plans trying to make sense of standards...

这个句子中有一个结构"make sense of"，表示"搞清……的意思"。去掉of，make sense表示讲得通，比如"That makes sense."表示那是讲得通的。

例 How do we make sense of these peculiar phenomena?
我们该如何弄清楚这些奇怪的现象呢？

④ On the other hand, right now there are amazing educators that are sharing information...

这个句子中有一个结构"on the other hand"，表示"在另一方面"。经常和"on the one hand"连用。连起来的意思为"在一方面……；在另一方面……"。

例 On the one hand, I want to go to the party. But on the other hand, I ought to be studying
一方面我想去派对，但是另一方面我应该学习。

经典名句 Famous Classics

1. Don't ever let somebody tell you can't do something. You got a dream, you got to protect it!
   别让别人告诉你，你成不了才！如果你有梦想的话，就要去捍卫！

2. When we step on the battlefield, I will be The First Boots On and the Last Boots Off.
   当我们踏上战场，我必将首先发起冲锋，也必然坚守到最后。

3. Whatever is worth doing is worth doing well.
   任何值得做的事就值得把它做好！

4. We are what we repeatedly do. Excellence, then, is not an act, but a habit.
   重复的行为造就了我们；因而，卓越不是一种举动，而是一种习惯。

5. Some people want it to happen, some wish it would happen, others make it happen.
   有些人想成功，还有些人渴望成功，另有些人通过努力使梦想成真。

读书笔记

05 Teach Teachers How to Create Magic B
老师如何创造魔力B

Christopher Emdin, science TED, October, 2013
克里斯托弗·艾姆丁在TED的演讲

The **reality** is, the folks I described as the master teachers, the master narrative builders, the master storytellers are far **removed** from classrooms. The folks who know the skills about how to teach and engage an audience don't even know what teacher **certification** means. They may not even have the degrees to be able to have anything to call an education. And that to me is sad. It's sad because the people who I described, they were very disinterested in the learning process, want to be **effective** teachers, but they have no models. I'm going to paraphrase Mark Twain. Mark Twain says that **proper** preparation, or teaching, is so powerful that it can turn bad morals to good, it can turn awful practices into powerful ones, it can change men and transform them into angels.

The folks who I described earlier got proper preparation in teaching, not in any college or university, but by **virtue**

实际上，我所描述的是教育大师、叙述大师、故事大师，而这些大师心里的课堂很遥远。那些掌握着如何教学并能够互动的人，甚至都不知道什么是教师资格证。或许他们都无法被人称之为教育者。这对于我来说，是件非常悲哀的事情。之所以是悲哀的事情，是因为我所描述的那些人，他们对学习的过程没兴趣，他们只想成为有效率的老师，但却没有成为范例。我要用马克·吐温的一句话表达。马克·吐温说适当的准备或教学，是非常强大的，可以将不好的品行变好，将糟糕的实践变得有趣，将改变人们，将他们改造为天使。

我之前说的那些有着适当教学准备的人，他们并不在大学里，他们只在有着同样兴趣的人中间，在可以产生互

of just being in the same spaces of those who engage. Guess where those places are? Barber shops, rap concerts, and most importantly, in the black church. And I've been framing this idea called Pentecostal pedagogy. Who here has been to a black church? We got a couple of hands. You go to a black church, their preacher starts off and he realizes that he has to engage the audience, so he starts off with this sort of wordplay in the beginning oftentimes, and then he takes a pause, and he says, "Oh my gosh, they're not quite paying attention." So he says, "Can I get an Amen?"

Audience: Amen.

Chris Emdin: So can I get an Amen? Audience: Amen.

CE: And all of a sudden, everybody's reawakened. That preacher bangs on the **pulpit** for attention. He drops his voice at a very, very low volume when he wants people to key into him, and those things are the skills that we need for the most engaging teachers. So why does teacher education only give you theory and theory and tell you about standards and tell you about all of these things that have nothing to do with the basic skills, that magic that you need to engage an audience, to engage a student? So I make the argument that we reframe teacher education, that we could focus

动的地方。猜猜在哪里呢？理发店，说唱音乐会，黑人教堂里。而我一直都在构造这个名为五旬节的教学法。有谁去过黑人教堂？有几个人。你们到一所黑人教堂，从他们做礼拜开始，就可以意识到他们需要吸引人的目光，因此他们就需要从文字游戏开始，然后突然停顿下来，并说："哦，天哪，他们注意力没有集中哟。"然后说："你们可以开始说阿门了吗？"

观众：阿门。

克里斯·艾姆丁：大家一起说"阿门"好吗？观众：阿门。

克里斯·艾姆丁：刹那间，人们都清醒了。那个牧师提高了传道的声音来吸引注意力。当他想要锁住人们的注意力时，就会刻意将声音放低。那些正是最能鼓舞人心的老师所必备的技能。为什么在教师培训时，只是不停地传授理论，告诉教学的标准，告诉你那些与基本技能无关的东西，这既不能鼓舞听众，也无法激励学生，是些没有魔力的东西。所以我立论：我们应该重塑师资培训，我们可以专注教学内容，我们可以专注教学理论，但是只有内容和理论是没有任何教与学的魔力的，那些

on content, and that's fine, and we could focus on theories, and that's fine, but content and theories with the **absence** of the magic of teaching and learning means nothing. 都是空谈。

单词解析 Word Analysis

reality [rɪ'ælɪtɪ] *n.* 现实

例 He escaped from reality by going to the cinema every afternoon.
他每天下午都去电影院，以此来逃避现实。

remove [rɪ'muːv] *v.* 移动；迁移

例 Will you remove your bag from the seat?
您能把您的包从座位上拿开吗？

certification [ˌsɜːtɪfɪ'keɪʃən] *n.* 证明；保证

例 We successfully got the certification for water diving.
我们成功地考下了潜水证。

effective [i'fektɪv] *adj.* 有效的；起作用的

例 The medicine is effective for curing the cold.
这种药治感冒很有效。

proper ['prɒpə] *adj.* 合适的；适当的

例 He didn't give me a proper answer for not showing up.
他没有给我一个不出现的恰当理由。

virtue ['vɜːtjuː] *n.* 美德；优点

例 Honesty is a virtue.
诚实是一种美德。

pulpit ['pʊlpɪt] *n.* 讲道坛；神职人员

例 He invited Sophie to the pulpit and prayed together.
他邀请苏菲到讲道坛，并且一起祈祷。

absence ['æbsəns] *n.* 缺席；缺乏

例 His team was wakened by his absence.
他的缺席导致小组实力的削弱。

语法知识点 Grammar Points

① **The master storytellers are far removed from classrooms.**

这个句子中有一个结构"remove sth. from..."，表示"移动；除掉；搬离"。

例 Can you find a way to remove the stain from the shirt?
你能想个办法去除衬衫上的污渍吗？

② **Teaching is so powerful that it can turn bad morals to good.**

这个句子中有两个结构："so...that..."，表示"如此……以至于……"；另一个结构是"turn...to..."，表示"将……变成……"。

例 This book was so interesting that I couldn't help finishing it within one hour.
这本书太有意思了，我止不住一小时就读完了它。

It was hard to believe that he turned stone to gold.
难以置信他竟然点石成金。

③ **Tell you about all of these things that have nothing to do with the basic skills...**

这个句子中有一个结构"have nothing to do with"，表示"与……无关"。反义词组是have something to do with，表示与……有关。

例 This traffic accident had nothing to do with him.
这起交通事故和他无关。

④ **We could focus on content.**

这个句子中有一个结构"focus on"，表示"全神贯注于……"。相同的结构有concentrate on和be absorbed in。

例 Students should focus on the study.
学生应该全神贯注于学习。

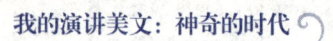

经典名句 Famous Classics

1. Everybody wants happiness. No one wants pain. But how can you make a rainbow without a little rain?
   大家都想得到幸福，却不愿承担痛苦。可不经历风雨，怎能见彩虹？

2. Never regret. If it's good, it's wonderful. If it's bad, it's experience.
   不必遗憾。若是美好，叫做精彩。若是糟糕，叫做经历。

3. The moment you think about giving up, think of the reason why you held on so long.
   每当你想放弃的时候，想一想是什么支撑着你一路坚持。

4. Time management is really a misnomer-the challenge is not to manage time, but to manage ourselves.
   时间管理其实是一个误称，我们挑战的是管理自己，而不是时间。

5. Don't worry too much about the ambiguous future, just make effort for explicit being present.
   不为模糊不清的未来过分担忧，只为清清楚楚的现在奋发图强。

读书笔记

06 Teach Teachers How to Create Magic C
老师如何创造魔力 C

Christopher Emdin, science TED, October, 2013
克里斯托弗·艾姆丁在 TED 的演讲

Now people often say, "Well, magic is just magic." There are teachers who, despite all their challenges, who have those skills, get into those schools and are able to engage an audience, and the **administrator** walks by and says, "Wow, he's so good, I wish all my teachers could be that good." And when they try to describe what that is, they just say, "He has that magic."

But I'm here to tell you that magic can be taught. Magic can be taught. Magic can be taught. Now, how do you teach it? You teach it by allowing people to go into those spaces where the magic is happening. If you want to be an aspiring teacher in urban education, you've got to leave the **confines** of that university and go into the hood. You've got to go in there and hang out at the barbershop, you've got to attend that black church, and you've got to view those folks that have the power to engage

人们常说："魔力只是魔力罢了。"只要老师不畏惧挑战，且拥有那些技能，就可以在学校激励和鼓舞学生。学校的管理者路过看到了会说："哇，他很会教学！我希望其他的老师可以和他一样优秀。"但是当他们谈论起他的教学为何成功时，他们只会说："他拥有魔力。"

但是我想告诉你们，那种魔力是可以教出来的。魔力是可以教的。但是怎么去使用呢？你可以让人们观看那些魔力产生的地方，传授这种技能。如果你想成为城市教育中一位有抱负的老师，你要走出大学的限制，进到魔力产生的地方。你要去理发店与人们交谈，去黑人教堂，去看看那些有感召力的人们，学习他们的做法。在我大学的教师培训课，我启动了一个项目，让每

025

and just take notes on what they do. At our teacher education classes at my university, I've started a **project** where every single student that comes in there sits and watches rap concerts. They watch the way that the rappers move and talk with their hands. They study the way that he walks proudly across that stage.

They listen to his metaphors and **analogies**, and they start learning these little things that, if they practice enough, become the key to magic. They learn that if you just stare at a student and raise your eyebrow about a quarter of an inch, you don't have to say a word because they know that that means that you want more. And if we could transform teacher education to focus on teaching teachers how to create that magic then poof! We could make dead classes come alive, we could **reignite** imaginations, and we can change education.

Thank you.

单词解析 Word Analysis

administrator [əd'mɪnɪstreɪtə] *n.* 管理人；行政官

例 You can do it only with the permission of the administrator.
只有在管理人同意的情况下你才可以做。

confine [kən'faɪn] *n.* 界限；约束 *v.* 限制；紧闭

例 She can't stand the confines of this marriage.
她无法忍受这个婚姻带来的限制。

Teach Teachers How to Create Magic C
老师如何创造魔力 C

project [prɒdʒekt] *n.* 工程；计划；事业 *v.* 计划；表达

例 Please count me in on this project.
请把我也算入这个项目的参加者。

analogy [əˈnælədʒɪ] *n.* 类比；对比

例 When I think about this situation, I always use the animal as an analogy.
当我想到这个情形的时候，我总是用动作来做类比。

reignite [riːɪɡˈnaɪt] *v.* 再次点燃；重新激起

例 The recent food-poisoning issue has reignited debate over the farming methods.
最近食物中毒事件再次激起了对于耕作方式的讨论。

语法知识点 Grammar Points

① There are teachers who, despite all their challenges, who have those skills, get into those schools and are able to engage an audience, and the administrator walks by and says, "Wow, he's so good, I wish all my teachers could be that good."

这个句子中有一个介词"despite"，表示"尽管如此；不管"。相当于短语in spite of。

例 He failed the test despite studying all night.
尽管整夜学习，他还是考试失败了。

② You teach it by allowing people to go into those spaces where the magic is happening.

这个句子中有一个结构"allow sb. to do."，表示"允许某人做某事"。如果直接接动词，动词搭配为allow doing。

例 They allowed their children to play in the park.
他们允许孩子们去公园玩。

③ You've got to go in there and hang out at the barbershop, you've got to attend that black church, and you've got to view those folks that have the power to engage and just take notes on what they do.

我的演讲美文：神奇的时代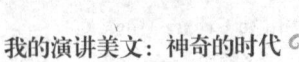

这个句子中有一个结构"hang out"，表示"闲逛；出去消遣"。

例 I used to hang out in the supermarket.
我过去常常在超市里闲逛。

④ They learn that if you just stare at a student and raise your eyebrow about a quarter of an inch...

这个句子中有一个结构"stare at"，表示"盯着"。和"看"相关的动词，一般都和介词at连用，例如glare at，表示怒视；glance at，表示瞥见。

例 She stared at me in surprise.
她惊奇地盯着我。

经典名句 Famous Classics

1. Things that make life easier: A parent's hug, a lover's kiss, a friend's support.
   让生活变轻松有三样东西：父母的拥抱，恋人的亲吻，朋友的支持。

2. If life is divided into two episodes, the first is "hesitance-free", while the second is "regret-free".
   若将人生一分为二，前半段叫"不犹豫"，后半段叫"不后悔"。

3. Let us face the reality, so that we are committed to our ideal. — Che Guevara
   让我们面对现实，让我们忠于理想。（切·格瓦拉）

4. If you wept for the missing sunset, you would miss all the shining stars.
   如果你为错过夕阳而哭泣，那么你就要错过群星了。

5. When it comes to going after what you love in life, don't take "NO" for an answer.
   当你追求人生所爱时，你的字典里就不该有"不可能"这个词。

07 Change with the World and Remake America A
与时俱进，重塑美国 A

Barack Obama
巴拉克·侯赛因·奥巴马，美国第44任总统

My fellow citizens:

I stand here today **humbled** by the task before us, grateful for the trust you have **bestowed**, mindful of the sacrifices borne by our ancestors. I thank President Bush for his service to our nation, as well as the generosity and cooperation he has shown throughout this transition.

Forty-four Americans have now taken the presidential oath. The words have been spoken during rising tides of prosperity and the still waters of peace. Yet, every so often, the oath is taken amidst gathering clouds and raging storms. At these moments, America has carried on not simply because of the skill or vision of those in high office, but because we the People have remained faithful to the ideals of our **forbearers**, and true to our founding documents.

So it has been. So it must be with this generation of Americans.

That we are in the midst of crisis

同胞们：

我今天站在这里，深感面前使命的重大，深谢你们赋予的信任，并铭记我们前辈所做的牺牲。我感谢布什总统对国家的贡献以及他在整个过渡阶段所展示出的慷慨协作。

至此，已有四十四位美国人发表过总统誓言。这些字词曾在蒸蒸日上的繁荣时期和宁静安详的和平年代被诵读。但是间或，它们也响彻在阴云密布、风暴降临的时刻。美国能够历经这些时刻而勇往直前，不仅因为当政者的远见卓识，也因为美国人民始终坚信我们先辈的理想，对我们的建国理念忠贞不渝。

前辈们如此，我们这一代美国人也更是如此。

现在我们深知，我们身处危机之中。我们的国家身处战争之中，打击分布广泛的暴力

is now well understood. Our nation is at war, against a far-reaching network of violence and hatred. Our economy is badly weakened, a consequence of greed and irresponsibility on the part of some, but also our collective failure to make hard choices and prepare the nation for a new age. Homes have been lost; jobs businesses **shutter**ed. Our health care is too costly; our schools fail too many; and each day brings further evidence that the ways we use energy strengthen our adversaries and threaten our planet.

These are the **indicator**s of crisis, subject to data and statistics. Less measurable but no less profound is a **sapping** of confidence across our land-a **nagging** fear that America's decline is inevitable, and that the next generation must lower its sights.

Today I say to you that the challenges we face are real. They are serious and they are many. They will not be met easily or in a short span of time. But know this, America: They will be met.

On this day, we gather because we have chosen hope over fear, unity of purpose over conflict and **discord**.

On this day, we come to proclaim an end to the petty grievances and false promises, the recriminations and worn-out **dogma**s, that for far too long have strangled our politics.

和仇恨势力。我们的经济严重衰退，原因虽有一些人的贪婪不轨，同时也是因为我们作为一个整体，未能痛下决心，让国家做好面对新时代的准备。如今，住房不在，就业减少，商业破产。医疗保健费用过度昂贵；学校质量没有保障；而每一天都在不断显示，我们使用能源的方式助长了我们的敌对势力，也威胁着我们的星球。

数据和统计都在预示着危机的来临。目前整个国家都面临信心动摇的问题，它虽不易衡量，却同样严重——这是一种挥之不去的恐惧感，认为美国将不可避免地走下坡路，下一代人不得不放低眼光。

今天，我告诉大家，我们面临的挑战真实存在，数量众多且情势严重。它们虽无法在短时间内被轻松解决。但是美国，请记住这句话——我们一定会渡过难关。

我们今天聚集在这里是因为我们选择希望而不是恐惧，选择齐心协力而不是冲突对立。

我们今天在这里宣告，让斤斤计较与虚假承诺就此结束，让窒息我国政治为时已久的相互指责和陈词滥调就此完结。

Change with the World and Remake America A
与时俱进，重塑美国 A

单词解析 *Word Analysis*

humble ['hʌmbl] *adj.* 谦逊的；简陋的；（级别或地位）低下的
- Defeat and failure make people humble.
  挫折与失败会使人谦卑。

bestow [bɪ'stəʊ] *v.* 使用；授予；放置；留宿
- The country bestowed its highest medal on the war hero.
  国家给战争英雄颁发国家最高奖章。

forbearer [fɔː'beə(r)] *n.* 祖先 *v.* 忍耐
- His forbearers ascend to the 15th century.
  他的祖先可上溯到十五世纪。

shutter ['ʃʌtə(r)] *v.* 装以遮门；关上窗板；停业
- The house was empty and shuttered.
  这所房子是空的，窗板都关上了。

indicator ['ɪndɪkeɪtə(r)] *n.* 指示器；指示剂；指示牌
- Complexion was thought to be an indicator of one's character.
  肤色被认为是一个人的性格的指示器。

sapping ['sæpɪŋ] *n.* 基蚀；挖掘；下切
- They wanted to draw us in to endless wars, sapping our strength and confidence as a nation.
  他们要把我们拖入无休止的战争中去，逐渐消耗完国民的力量和信心。

nagging ['nægɪŋ] *adj.* 唠叨的；挑剔的；使人不得安宁的 *n.* 唠叨；挑剔
- I can't stomach your constant nagging.
  我再也忍受不了你不停的唠叨了。

discord ['dɪskɔːd] *n.* 不和；不调和；嘈杂声
- His remark discords with the fact.
  他的话与事实不符。

dogma ['dɒgmə] *n.* 教条，教理；武断的意见
- It is precisely such ignorant people who take Marxism-Leninism

as a religious dogma.
那些将马克思列宁主义当宗教教条看待的人，就是这种蒙昧无知的人。

语法知识点 Grammar Points

① **Forty-four Americans have now taken the presidential oath.**

这个句子中有一个结构"take the oath"，表示"宣誓"，等同于swear。

例 As he prepares to take the oath of office, Barack Obama's biggest political roadblock may end up being institutional hurdles rather than a united Republican opposition.
竞选总统奥巴马正在为宣誓就职做准备，然而制度的阻碍有可能成为他最大的政治障碍，而并非是共和党的联合对抗。

② **...but because we the People have remained faithful to the ideals of our forbearers...**

这个句子中有一个结构"(be) faithful to"，表示"忠诚于"，等同于be true to。

例 It has been so much my religion ever since we were married to be faithful to you in every thought and look.
自从我们结婚以来，我的宗教就是在思想上和外表上都要忠实于你。

③ **Our nation is at war, against a far-reaching network of violence and hatred.**

这个句子中有一个结构"be at war"，表示"处于战争中"。

例 We have spent over a trillion dollars at war, often financed by borrowing from overseas.
我们在战争中的耗费超过一万亿美元，而且经常从国外借贷资金。

④ **These are the indicators of crisis, subject to data and statistics.**

这个句子中有一个结构"(be) subject to"，表示"服从，受……支配，取决于……"。

例 Although these targets would not be internationally binding, they would be subject to outside verification.
虽然这些目标不具有国际约束力，但它们将受到外界监督。

经典名句 Famous Classics

1. Knowledge is power. Information is liberating. Education is the premise of progress, in every society, in every family.
   知识是力量,资讯是救赎,教育是进步的前提,在每一个社会及家庭。

2. If you are not criticized, you may not be doing much.
   要是都没有人批评你,表示你可能没做什么事。

3. The greatest of faults, I should say, is to be conscious of none.
   我必须说,最大的过错,莫过于看不到任何过错。

4. Most of our obstacles would melt away if instead of cowering before them we should make up our minds to walk boldly through them.
   与其在困难面前蜷缩起来,不如勇敢地从它中间穿过,大部分的困难都可迎刃而解。

5. Find a group of people who challenge and inspire you; spend a lot of time with them, and it will change your life.
   找一群会刺激并鼓舞你的人,花很多时间和他们在一起,这将改变你的人生。

08 Change with the World and Remake America B
与时俱进，重塑美国 B

Barack Obama
巴拉克·侯赛因·奥巴马，美国第44任总统

We remain a young nation, but in the words of Scripture, the time has come to set aside childish things. The time has come to **reaffirm** our enduring spirit; to choose our better history; to carry forward that precious gift, that noble idea, passed on from generation to generation: the God-given promise that all are equal, all are free, and all **deserve** a chance to pursue their full measure of happiness.

In reaffirming the greatness of our nation, we understand that greatness is never a given. It must be earned. Our journey has never been one of shortcuts or settling for less. It has not been the path for the **fainthearted**-for those who prefer leisure over work, or seek only the pleasures of riches and fame. Rather, it has been the risk-takers, the doers, the makers of things-some celebrated, but more often men and women obscure in their labor-who have carried us up the

我们仍是一个年轻的国家，但如圣经所言，抛弃幼稚的时刻已经到来。重拾坚韧精神的时刻已经到来，我们要做出更好的历史选择，我们要秉承历史赋予的宝贵权利，秉承代代相传的高贵理想：上帝赋予所有人平等、自由和充分追求幸福的机会。

在重申我们国家伟大之处的同时，我们深知，伟大并非从天而降，而需努力赢得。我们一路走来，从未谋求捷径或退而求其次。这旅途不属于弱者——它不属于好逸恶劳或只图名利享受之徒；这条路属于冒险者、实干家和创造者——这些人有些名留青史，但大多数是默默无闻耕耘劳作的男女志士，是他们带我们走向通往繁荣和自由的漫长崎岖之路。

为了我们，他们打点起贫寒的行装上路，远赴重洋，追

Change with the World and Remake America B
与时俱进，重塑美国 B 08

long, **rugged** path toward prosperity and freedom.

For us, they packed up their few worldly possessions and traveled across oceans in search of a new life.

For us, they **toiled** in **sweatshops** and settled the West; endured the **lash** of the whip and **plowed** the hard earth.

For us, they fought and died, in places like Concord and Gettysburg; Normandy and Khe Sahn.

Time and again, these men and women struggled and sacrificed and worked till their hands were raw so that we might live a better life. They saw America as bigger than the sum of our individual ambitions; greater than all the differences of birth or wealth or faction.

This is the journey we continue today. We remain the most prosperous, powerful nation on Earth. Our workers are no less productive than when this crisis began. Our minds are no less inventive, our goods and services no less needed than they were last week or last month or last year. Our capacity remains **undiminished**. But our time of standing pat, of protecting narrow interests and putting off unpleasant decisions-that time has surely passed. Starting today, we must pick ourselves up, dust ourselves off, and begin again the work of remaking America.

求新生活。

为了我们，他们用血汗浇铸工厂，在西部原野拓荒，忍着鞭笞之痛在坚硬的土地上耕耘。

为了我们，他们奔赴疆场，英勇捐躯，长眠于康科德、葛底斯堡、诺曼底和溪山。

为了我们能够过上更好的生活，他们前赴后继，历尽艰辛，全力奉献，不辞劳苦，直至双手结起层层老茧。在他们看来，美国的强盛与伟大超越了个人的雄心壮志，也超越了所有种族、财富或派系的差异。

今天，我们踏上了先人们这一未竟的旅程。我们依然是地球上最富裕、最强大的国家。与危机初露端倪之时相比，我们的劳动者生产力依然旺盛；我们的头脑依然富于创造力。我们的产品与服务仍旧受欢迎如往昔。我们的实力丝毫未损。但是，维持现状、保护狭隘的时代、对艰难决定犹豫不决的时代无疑已成为过去。从今天起，我们必须振作起来，拍拍我们身上的尘土，重新开始，重塑美国的事业。

我们目之所及，都有工作等待着我们。经济形势要求我们果敢而迅速地行动，我们的确要行动——不仅要创造新的就业机会，而且要打下新的增

For everywhere we look, there is work to be done. The state of the economy calls for action, bold and swift, and we will act-not only to create new jobs, but to lay a new foundation for growth. We will build the roads and bridges, the electric grids and digital lines that feed our commerce and bind us together. We will **restore** science to its rightful place, and wield technology's wonders to raise health care's quality and lower its cost. We will harness the sun and the winds and the soil to fuel our cars and run our factories. And we will transform our schools and colleges and universities to meet the demands of a new age. All this we can do. And all this we will do.

Now, there are some who question the scale of our ambitions-who suggest that our system cannot tolerate too many big plans. Their memories are short. For they have forgotten what this country has already done; what free men and women can achieve when imagination is joined to common purpose, and necessity to courage.

长基础。我们将造桥铺路，架设电网，为企业铺设电网和数字线路。我们将回归科学，利用高新技术的超常潜力提高医疗保健质量并降低成本。我们将利用太阳能、风力和地热驱动车辆，为工厂提供能源。我们将改革我们的中小学及大专院校，以应对新时代的挑战。这一切我们都能做到，这一切我们必将做到。

现在，有人开始质疑我们的雄心壮志——他们说我们的体制不能承受太多的宏伟规划。他们是健忘的，因为他们忘记了这个国家已经取得的成就，忘记了一旦共同的目标插上理想的翅膀、现实的要求鼓起勇气的风帆，自由的人民就会爆发出无穷的创造力。

单词解析 *Word Analysis*

reaffirm [ˌriːəˈfɜːm] 重申，再确认

例 It is particularly important to reaffirm this point today.
今天重申这一点，有特别重要的意义。

Change with the World and Remake America B
与时俱进，重塑美国 B

deserve [dɪ'zɜːv] *v.* 应受，值得

例 He has done nothing to deserve death.
他没做过该受死刑的事。

fainthearted ['feɪnth'ɑːtɪd] *adj.* 懦弱的；无精神的；胆小的

例 A fearful person is a fainthearted person.
怕这怕那的人是软弱的人。

rugged ['rʌgɪd] *adj.* 高低不平的；崎岖的；粗犷的；粗鲁的；（人）坚毅的；（气候）严酷的；（声音）刺耳的；坚固耐用的

例 They walk on the rugged country road.
他们在崎岖不平的乡村小路上走着。

toil [tɔɪl] *n.* 辛苦；苦工；罗网；圈套 *v.* 费力地做；苦干；跋涉

例 We were quite exhausted with the toil.
我们因那件辛苦的工作而感到十分疲惫。

sweatshop ['swetʃɒp] *n.* 血汗工厂（工作条件恶劣而工资低的工厂）

例 He spent three years in a sweatshop before he found a decent job.
他在一家血汗工厂做了三年才找到一份像样的工作。

lash [læʃ] *n.* 鞭子；鞭打；睫毛；讽刺 *v.* 鞭打；摆动；抨击

例 He began to lash Luke unmercifully across buttocks and thighs.
他开始无情地鞭打卢克的屁股和大腿。

plow [plaʊ] *n.* 犁；耕地 *v.* 耕犁；费力通过；破浪前行

例 He teamed one horse and one cow to a plow.
他把一匹马和一头牛套在犁上。

undiminished [ˌʌndɪ'mɪnɪʃt] *adj.* 不减的；未衰落的；没有降低的

例 They continued with undiminished enthusiasm.
他们热情依旧地继续着。

restore [rɪ'stɔː(r)] *v.* 恢复；归还；复原

例 The military government promised to restore democracy within one year.
军人政府答应在一年内重新建立民主体制。

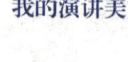

语法知识点 Grammar Points

① ...the time has come to set aside childish things.

这个句子中有一个结构"set aside",表示"把……放到一边,留出"。

例 They work hard, marry, have lots of children and set aside an evening each week for quality time with the family.
他们努力工作,结婚,生许多小孩,每周都会留出一个晚上来和家人讨论与家庭、孩子有关的话题。

② ...these men and women struggled and sacrificed and worked till their hands were raw so that we might live a better life.

这个句子中有一个结构"live a ...life",表示"过……的生活"。

例 Would you want to live a life on the experience machine?
你想在体验机里生活吗?

③ But our time of standing pat, of protecting narrow interests and putting off unpleasant decisions...

这个句子中有一个结构"put off",表示"推迟,扔掉,阻止",等同于postpone和delay。Delay多指因外界原因推迟或耽误,也可指有意推迟。Postpone是正式用词,语气较强,多指有安排的延期,常指明延期到一定的时间。

例 We've invited friends to supper and it's too late to put them off now.
我已邀请朋友来吃晚饭,现在取消已来不及了。

④ ...not only to create new jobs, but to lay a new foundation for growth.

这个句子中有一个结构"lay a foundation for...",表示"奠定基础"。

例 Lay the foundation for future growth.
为未来发展打下基础。

经典名句 Famous Classics

1. The task of leadership is not to put greatness into humanity, but to elicit it, for the greatness is already there.

领导者的工作不是把卓越注入人类，而是把它引发出来，因为卓越原本就在。

2. Act the way you'd like to be and soon you'll be the way you act.
   以你想要的方式行动，很快你就会成为那个样子。

3. The goal is not always meant to be reached, but to serve as a mark for our aim.
   目标不一定永远都会达到，但可以当我们瞄准的方向。

4. From error to error one discovers the entire truth.
   经由一次次的犯错，我们得以发现整个真相。

5. Some men give up their designs when they have almost reached the goal; while others, on the contrary, obtain a victory by exerting, at the last moment, more vigorous efforts than ever before.
   有些人在几乎要达成目标时会放弃他们的设想；而另一些人则相反，在最后一刻比以往更积极努力地去获取胜利。

读书笔记

09 Change with the World and Remake America C
与时俱进，重塑美国 C

Barack Obama
巴拉克·侯赛因·奥巴马，美国第44任总统

What the **cynics** fail to understand is that the ground has shifted beneath them-that the **stale** political arguments that have **consumed** us for so long no longer apply. The question we ask today is not whether our government is too big or too small, but whether it works-whether it helps families find jobs at a decent wage, care they can afford, a retirement that is dignified. Where the answer is yes, we intend to move forward. Where the answer is no, programs will end. And those of us who manage the public's dollars will be held to account-to spend wisely, reform bad habits, and do our business in the light of day-because only then can we restore the **vital** trust between a people and their government.

Nor is the question before us whether the market is a force for good or ill. Its power to generate wealth and expand freedom is unmatched, but this

那些冷眼旁观的人没有认识到他们脚下的大地已经移动——那些长期以来空耗我们精力的陈腐政治观点已经过时。我们今天提出的问题不在于我们的政府大小，而是它是否行之有效——它是否能够帮助人们找到报酬合理的就业机会，是否能够为他们提供费用适度的医疗保健服务，是否能够确保他们在退休后不失尊严。如果回答是肯定的，我们就要向前推进。如果回答是否定的，计划和项目必须终止。作为公共资金的管理者，我们必须承担责任——明智地使用资金，抛弃陋习，在阳光下履行职责——因为只有这样我们才能重建人民对政府至关重要的信任。

我们提出的问题也不在于市场力量是替天行道还是为虎作伥。市场在生成财富和

crisis has reminded us that without a watchful eye, the market can **spin** out of control-and that a nation cannot **prosper** long when it favors only the prosperous. The success of our economy has always depended not just on the size of our gross domestic product, but on the reach of our prosperity; on our ability to extend opportunity to every willing heart-not out of charity, but because it is the surest route to our common good.

As for our common defense, we reject as false the choice between our safety and our ideals. Our Founding Fathers, faced with **perils** we can **scarcely** imagine, drafted a charter to assure the rule of law and the rights of man, a charter expanded by the blood of generations. Those ideals still light the world, and we will not give them up for **expedience**'s sake. And so to all other peoples and governments who are watching today, from the grandest capitals to the small village where my father was born: Know that America is a friend of each nation and every man, woman and child who seeks a future of peace and **dignity**, and that we are ready to lead once more.

传播自由方面具有无与伦比的力量，但这场危机提醒我们：没有严格的监督，市场就会失控——如果一个国家仅仅施惠于富裕者，其富裕便不能持久。我们的经济成功从来不是仅仅依赖国内总产值的规模，而是依赖繁荣的普及，即为每一位希望致富的人提供机会的能力——我们这样做并非出自恻隐之心，而是因为这是我们实现共同利益的必由之路。

至于我们的共同防御，我们决不接受安全与理想不可两全的荒谬论点。建国先贤面对我们难以想见的险恶局面，起草了一部保障法治和人权的宪章，一部子孙后代用鲜血扩展充实的宪章。今天，这些理念仍然照耀着世界，我们不会为一时之利而弃之。因此，对于今天正在观看此情此景的其他各国人民和政府——从最繁华的首都到我父亲出生的小村庄——我们希望他们了解：凡是追求和平与尊严的国家以及每一位男人、妇女和儿童，美国是你们的朋友。我们已经做好准备，再一次引领大家。

单词解析 *Word Analysis*

cynic ['sɪnɪk] *n.* 愤世嫉俗者；悲观者；犬儒主义者；好挖苦的人 *adj.* 犬儒学派的；好讥讽的

例 I'm too much of a cynic to believe that he'll keep his promise.
我太愤世嫉俗了，不能相信他会遵守诺言。

stale [steɪl] *adj.* 不新鲜的；陈腐的；厌倦的 *v.* 变得不新鲜；腐坏；（动物）撒尿

例 His hunger makes his stale bread go down.
饥饿使他把这不新鲜的面包吞了下去。

consume [kən'sju:m] *v.* 消耗；吃喝；毁灭

例 His old car consumed much gasoline.
他的旧汽车耗油很多。

vital ['vaɪtl] *adj.* 至关重要的；有活力的；生死攸关的

例 The government saw the introduction of new technology as vital.
政府认为引进新技术至关重要。

spin [spɪn] *v.* （使）旋转；疾驰；纺织；结网；眩晕 *n.* 纺织；旋转；眩晕；疾驰

例 My sister can spin on her toes like a dancer.
我妹妹能像舞者一样踮着脚尖旋转。

prosper ['prɒspə(r)] *v.* 繁盛；成功；兴旺

例 We are bound to prosper beyond other countries.
我们肯定要比其他国家更兴旺繁荣。

peril ['perəl] *n.* 危险；冒险 *v.* 冒险

例 These birds are able to survive the perils of the Arctic winter.
这些鸟能在北极寒冷的冬天里生存。

scarcely ['skeəsli] *adv.* 几乎不；简直不；刚刚；决不

例 He spoke scarcely a word of English.
他几乎连一个英文单词都不会说。

expedience [ɪkˈspɪdɪəns] *n.* 便利；权宜之计；私利

例 The expedience of war opened the doors to American drug traffic and Mafia domination.
战争的私利就是给美军的毒品交易和黑手党打开大门。

dignity [ˈdɪgnəti] *n.* 尊严；高贵；端庄

例 He would do nothing beneath his dignity.
他决不愿意干任何有损自身尊严的事。

语法知识点 Grammar Points

① **What the cynics fail to understand is that the ground has shifted beneath them...**

这个句子中有一个结构 "fail to do..."，表示 "做某事失败了"。

例 Those who have tried to do sth. but fail are much stronger than those who have tried nothing but succeed.
那些尝试去做某事却失败的人，比那些什么也不尝试做却成功的人不知要好上多少。

② **The success of our economy has always depended not just on the size of our gross domestic product...**

这个句子中有一个结构 "depend on"，表示 "依靠"，相当于depend upon和rely on/upon。

例 My wife and daughter depend on me for their living.
我妻子女儿靠我生活。

③ **...and we will not give them up for expedience's sake.**

这个句子中有一个结构 "for one's sake"，表示 "为……起见，为了……的利益"。

例 He tried to assure me that he wouldn't lie just for one dollar's sake.
他向我保证他不会为了一美元而讲假话。

经典名句 *Famous Classics*

1. Life is like a game of cards. The hand you are dealt is determinism; the way you play it is free will.
   人生宛如一场牌局，拿到什么牌，那是命中注定，但如何出牌，却操之在己。

2. All that I am, or hope to be, I owe to my angel mother.
   我的一切，以及我渴望成为的那个人，都拜我仁慈的母亲之赐。

3. You must have long-range goals to keep you from being frustrated by short-term failures.
   你必须要有远期目标，以让你在短期失败时不致感到受挫。

4. The quality of a leader is reflected in the standards they set for themselves.
   一个领导者的本质，反映在他们为自己定立的标准。

5. Just as people behave to me, so do I behave to them. When I see that a person despises me and treats me with contempt, I can be as proud as any peacock.
   别人怎样对待我，我也可以怎样对待他们，如果有人瞧不起我或轻蔑地对待我，我也可以让自己骄傲得像孔雀一样。

读书笔记

10 Change with the World and Remake America D
与时俱进，重塑美国 D

Barack Obama
巴拉克·侯赛因·奥巴马，美国第44任总统

Recall that earlier generations faced down **fascism** and **communism** not just with **missiles** and tanks, but with **sturdy** alliances and enduring convictions. They understood that our power alone cannot protect us, nor does it **entitle** us to do as we please. Instead, they knew that our power grows through its prudent use; our security **emanates** from the justness of our cause, the force of our example, the **tempering** qualities of humility and restraint.

We are the keepers of this legacy. Guided by these principles once more, we can meet those new threats that demand even greater effort-even greater cooperation and understanding between nations. We will begin to responsibly leave Iraq to its people, and forge a hard earned peace in Afghanistan. With old friends and former **foes**, we will work tirelessly to lessen the nuclear threat, and roll back the **specter** of a warming

回顾过去，几代人在战胜法西斯主义时依靠的不仅仅是导弹和坦克，更是牢固的联盟和不渝的信念。他们懂得单凭实力无法保护我们的安全，实力也并不赋予我们随心所欲的权利。相反，他们知道审慎使用实力会使我们更强大；我们的安全源于事业的正义性、榜样的感召力，以及谦卑和克制的平衡作用。

我们是这一传统的继承者。我们只要重新以这些原则为指导，就能应对那些新威胁，为此必须付出更大的努力——推动国家间更多合作，加深彼此理解。我们会开始以负责任的方式把伊拉克移交给伊拉克人民，并在阿富汗巩固来之不易的和平。我们将与多年旧友和昔日对手一道不懈努力，减轻核威胁，扭转全球变暖的厄运。我们不会在价值观

planet. We will not apologize for our way of life, nor will we **waver** in its defense, and for those who seek to advance their aims by inducing terror and slaughtering innocents, we say to you now that our spirit is stronger and cannot be broken; you cannot outlast us, and we will defeat you.

For we know that our patchwork heritage is a strength, not a weakness. We are a nation of Christians and Muslims, Jews and Hindus-and nonbelievers. We are shaped by every language and culture, drawn from every end of this Earth; and because we have tasted the bitter swill of civil war and segregation, and emerged from that dark chapter stronger and more united, we cannot help but believe that the old hatreds shall someday pass; that the lines of tribe shall soon dissolve; that as the world grows smaller, our common humanity shall reveal itself; and that America must play its role in ushering in a new era of peace.

念上退缩，也不会动摇捍卫它的决心，对于那些妄图以煽动恐怖和屠杀无辜的手段达到其目的之人，我们现在向你们宣告：我们的意志更加顽强、坚不可摧；你们无法拖垮我们，我们必将战胜你们。

因为我们知道，我们百纳而成的传统是一种优势，而非劣势。我们是一个由基督教徒和穆斯林、犹太教徒和印度教徒，以及无宗教信仰者组成的国家。我们受惠于地球上四面八方每一种语言和文化的影响。由于我们饮过南北战争和种族隔离的苦水，涅槃自那个黑暗时代，变得更加坚强和团结，我们坚信昔日的仇恨终有一天会成为过去；部族之间的界线很快会消失；随着世界变得越来越小，我们共同的人性将得到彰显；美国必将发挥作用，迎来一个和平的新纪元。

单词解析 *Word Analysis*

fascism ['fæʃɪzəm] *n.* 法西斯主义；独裁统治

例 Fascism is the most ruthless enemy of the people.
法西斯主义是人民最残酷无情的敌人。

Change with the World and Remake America D
与时俱进，重塑美国 D

communism ['kɒmjunɪzəm] *n.* 共产主义
- Communism is based on Marxism.
  共产主义是以马克思主义为基础。

missile ['mɪsaɪl] *n.* 导弹；投射物
- The missile deflected from its trajectory.
  导弹已偏离轨道。

sturdy ['stɜːdi] *adj.* 强健的；坚固的；坚决的
- The sturdy young man removed the rock without effort.
  那个壮实的小伙子没费多大劲便把石块搬开了。

entitle [ɪn'taɪtl] *v.* 取名为；使有权利
- She read a poem entitled *The Apple Tree*.
  她读了一首题为《苹果树》的诗。

emanate ['eməneɪt] *v.* 散发；发出
- Soul Power is a power that can only emanate from within.
  只有灵魂力量是从内在发出的。

temper ['tempə(r)] *n.* 脾气；性情 *v.* 使缓和；调和；锻炼
- He slammed the door in a temper.
  他生气地摔门。

foe [fəʊ] *n.* 敌人；仇敌
- The knight was murdered by his foes.
  那位骑士被他的敌人谋杀了。

specter ['spektə] *n.* 幽灵；妖怪；恐怖的根源
- The specter of unemployment hunted the country.
  失业的幽灵在这个国家作祟。

waver ['weɪvə(r)] *v.* 动摇；摇曳；犹豫；颤抖 *n.* 动摇；踌躇；挥动者；烫发器
- They did not waver in their support for him.
  他们毫不动摇地支持他。

语法知识点 Grammar Points

① We will begin to responsibly leave Iraq to its people...

这个句子中有一个结构"leave sth. to sb.",表示"把某物留给某人"。

例 The dean left this matter (up) to me.
系主任把这件事交给我处理。

② ...and for those who seek to advance their aims by inducing terror and slaughtering innocents...

这个句子中有一个结构"seek to",表示"追寻,争取",等同于pursue。

例 Any people in their lifetime avoid or do not even seek to find the answer to that question.
许多人在他们的一生中都在逃避或根本没有去寻找过这个问题的答案。

③ ...and that America must play its role in ushering in a new era of peace.

这个句子中有一个结构"usher in",表示"引领,引进"。

例 If art and light usher in calm, then for one week each year, the Old City of Jerusalem fosters that aura.
如果艺术和灯光引进了平静的理念,那么每年一周,这座古老的城市——耶路撒冷就形成了那种氛围。

经典名句 Famous Classics

1. Change does not roll in on the wheels of inevitability, but comes through continuous struggle.
改变不是如不可避免的轮子般滚进来,而是通过持续的挣扎奋斗。

2. Jealousy contains more of self-love than of love.
嫉妒藏着对自己的爱多于对他人的爱。

3. The way I see it, if you want the rainbow, you've got to put up with the rain.
我的看法是,如果你想要彩虹,就要能承受下雨。

4. As a well spent day brings happy sleep, so life well used brings happy death.
好好利用白天可让人欣慰地入睡，好好利用人生可让人欣慰地离世。

5. When people hurt you over and over, think of them like sandpaper. They may scratch and hurt you a bit, but in the end, you end up polished and they end up useless.
如果有人一再伤害你，就把他们当做砂纸，他们可能会刮伤你，但最终你会变得更圆滑，他们则变得没有用处。

读书笔记

11 Change with the World and Remake America E
与时俱进，重塑美国 E

Barack Obama
巴拉克·侯赛因·奥巴马，美国第44任总统

To the Muslim world, we seek a new way forward, based on mutual interest and mutual respect. To those leaders around the globe who seek to sow **conflict**, or blame their society's ills on the West: Know that your people will judge you on what you can build, not what you destroy. To those who cling to power through **corruption** and **deceit** and the silencing of **dissent**, know that you are on the wrong side of history; but that we will extend a hand if you are willing to **unclench** your fist.

To the people of poor nations, we **pledge** to work alongside you to make your farms flourish and let clean waters flow; to nourish starved bodies and feed hungry minds. And to those nations like ours that enjoy relative plenty, we say we can no longer afford indifference to suffering outside our borders; nor can we consume the world's resources without regard to effect. For the world has

面对穆斯林世界，我们寻求一条新的前进道路，以共同利益和相互尊重为基础。对于世界上那些妄图制造矛盾、将自己社会的弊端归罪于西方的领导人，我们奉劝你们：你们人民的评判将基于你们的成就，而非毁灭。对于那些依靠腐败、欺骗、压制不同意见等手段固守权势的人，我们提醒你们：你们站在了历史错误的一边；但只要你们放弃压迫，我们将伸手相助。

对于贫困国家的人民，我们保证同你们并肩努力，为你们的农田带来丰收，让清洁的用水取之不竭；使饥饿的身体得以饱食，使饥渴的心灵受到滋润。对于那些如我们一样相对富裕的国家，我们要说我们再不能对他人的苦难无动于衷，也再不能肆意消耗世界的资源。世界已经改变，我们必

changed, and we must change with it.

As we consider the road that unfolds before us, we remember with humble gratitude those brave Americans who, at this very hour, **patrol** far-off deserts and distant mountains. They have something to tell us today, just as the fallen heroes who lie in Arlington **whisper** through the ages. We honor them not only because they are guardians of our liberty, but because they embody the spirit of service; a willingness to find meaning in something greater than themselves. And yet, at this moment-a moment that will define a generation-it is precisely this spirit that must **inhabit** us all.

For as much as government can do and must do, it is ultimately the faith and determination of the American people upon which this nation relies. It is the kindness to take in a stranger when the levees break, the selflessness of workers who would rather cut their hours than see a friend lose their job which sees us through our darkest hours. It is the firefighter's courage to storm a **stairway** filled with smoke, but also a parent's willingness to nurture a child, that finally decides our fate.

须与时俱进。

在思索我们面前的道路时，我们怀着崇敬的心情感谢此刻正在偏远的沙漠和山区巡逻的英勇无畏的美国人。他们有话要说，正如在阿灵顿公墓长眠的阵亡英雄在漫漫岁月中低浅的吟诵。我们崇敬他们，因为他们不仅捍卫我们的自由，而且是服务精神的化身，他们超越个人，追寻更远大的理想。然而，在这个时刻，这个具有划时代意义的时刻，我们大家必须具备的正是这种精神。

虽然政府能有许多作为也必须有许多作为，但最终离不开美国人民的信仰和决心，这便是我国的立国之本。正是因为人们在大堤崩裂时接纳陌生人的关爱之情，正是因为工人们宁愿减少自己的工时而不愿看到朋友失去工作的无私精神，才使我们度过了最暗淡的时光。正是因为消防队员们有勇气冲进浓烟滚滚的楼道，也正是因为父母培养孩子成人的意愿，这些才是最终决定我们命运之事。

单词解析 *Word Analysis*

conflict [ˈkɒnflɪkt] *n.* 冲突；战斗；矛盾；斗争 *v.* 冲突；抵触；争执

例 He was wounded in the conflict.
他在战斗中负伤。

corruption [kəˈrʌpʃn] *n.* 贪污；堕落；腐败

例 Accusations of corruption have been made against him.
对他贪污的控告已经提出。

deceit [dɪˈsiːt] *n.* 欺骗；诡计；不诚实

例 She told him of his old mother's deceit.
她向他诉说了他的老母亲的欺骗行为。

dissent [dɪˈsent] *n.* 异议 *v.* 持异议

例 They expressed their dissent from official policy.
他们对官方的政策表示出异议。

unclench [ˌʌnˈklentʃ] *v.* 弄开；撬开；松开

例 As the President said in his inaugural address, we will hold out our hand-they have to unclench their fist.
正如总统在他的就职讲话里说的，我们将会伸出我们的手，他们需要松开他们的拳头。

pledge [pledʒ] *v.* 发誓；保证；以……抵押；向……祝酒 *n.* 保证；抵押；誓言；抵押品

例 They pledged never to tell the secret.
他们发誓决不泄密。

patrol [pəˈtrəʊl] *n.* 巡逻；巡查 *v.* 巡逻；巡查

例 Terrorists attacked two soldiers on patrol.
恐怖分子袭击了两名正在巡逻的士兵。

whisper [ˈwɪspə(r)] *n.* 低语；窃窃私语；飒飒的声音 *v.* 耳语；私语

例 There is no word, no whisper, no cry.
这里没有消息，没有低语，没有呼唤。

inhabit [ɪnˈhæbɪt] *v.* 居住于；占据；栖息

例 Wookiees inhabit the upper levels of the forest, having built their massive cities within the interwoven canopy.
伍基人占据了树林的上层，并在交织的树冠上建造了巨大的城市。

stairway [ˈsteəweɪ] *n.* 楼梯

例 Tongues of flame leaped up the stairway.
火舌沿楼梯迅速向上蔓延。

语法知识点 Grammar Points

① ...we seek a new way forward, based on mutual interest and mutual respect.

这个句子中有一个结构"base on"，表示"基于，在……基础上"。

例 The development is based on the information.
发展基于信息。

② ...or blame their society's ills on the West...

这个句子中有一个结构"blame sth. on sb."，表示"将某事归咎于某人"。另外sb. be to blame是指某人应该接受惩罚或者责任。

例 The police blame the accident on the driver who was attempting to pass.
警方把事故的责任归咎于当时极力驶过去的司机。

③ To those who cling to power through corruption and deceit and the silencing of dissent...

这个句子中有一个结构"cling to"，表示"坚持，依靠，依附"。同义词组还有stick to和hold on to。

例 The mud clung to my shoes.
泥粘在我的鞋子上。

经典名句 Famous Classics

1. Most great people have attained their greatest success one step

beyond their greatest failure.
多数的杰出者，是在他们最大的失败的下一步取得他们最大的成功。

2. Until you're ready to look foolish, you'll never have the possibility of being great.
除非你准备好看来愚蠢，你永远不会有机会变得伟大。

3. Always do your best. What you plant now, you will harvest later.
永远全力以赴，今日播下的种子，终会得到丰收。

4. Dream big and dare to fail.
敢于梦想并敢于失败。

5. It is better to be hated for what you are than to be loved for what you are not.
宁可人恶真我，不愿人喜假我。

读书笔记

12 Change with the World and Remake America F
与时俱进，重塑美国 F

Barack Obama
巴拉克·侯赛因·奥巴马，美国第44任总统

Our challenges may be new. The **instrument**s with which we meet them may be new. But those values upon which our success depends-hard work and honesty, courage and fair play, **tolerance** and curiosity, loyalty and **patriotism**-these things are old. These things are true. They have been the quiet force of progress throughout our history. What is demanded then is a return to these truths. What is required of us now is a new era of responsibility-a **recognition**, on the part of every American, that we have duties to ourselves, our nation and the world; duties that we do not **grudging**ly accept but rather seize gladly, firm in the knowledge that there is nothing so satisfying to the spirit, so defining of our character, than giving our all to a difficult task.

This is the price and the promise of **citizenship**.

This is the source of our confidence-

我们面临的挑战可能前所未闻。我们迎接挑战的方式也可能前所未有。然而，我们赖以成功的价值观——诚实和勤奋、勇气和公平、宽容心和探索精神、忠诚和爱国——均由来已久。这些价值观都千真万确。这些价值观是美国历史过程中一股无声的进步力量。现在需要的便是重归这些真理。我们现在需要开创负责任的新时代——每一位美国人都需要认识到我们对自己、对国家、对全世界都负有义务。对于这些义务，我们并非勉强接受，而是主动乐于承担，同时坚信我们为艰巨的使命付出一切，没有任何事可以如此满足我们的道义感，也没有任何事能如此体现我们的特性。

这就是公民的义务和承诺。

这就是我们信心的来源——知道上帝召唤我们：纵

the knowledge that God calls on us to shape an uncertain destiny. This is the meaning of our liberty and our **creed**- why men and women and children of every race and every faith can join in celebration across this magnificent Mall, and why a man whose father less than 60 years ago might not have been served at a local restaurant can now stand before you to take a most **sacred** oath.

So let us mark this day with **remembrance**, of who we are and how far we have traveled. In the year of America's birth, in the coldest of months, a small band of patriots **huddle**d by dying campfires on the shores of an icy river. The capital was abandoned. The enemy was advancing. The snow was stained with blood. At a moment when the outcome of our revolution was most in doubt, the father of our nation ordered these words be read to the people: "Let it be told to the future world...that in the depth of winter, when nothing but hope and virtue could survive...that the city and the country, alarmed at one common danger, came forth to meet it."

America. In the face of our common dangers, in this winter of our hardship, let us remember these timeless words. With hope and virtue, let us brave once more the icy currents, and endure what storms may come. Let it be said by our children's

然前路未卜，命运也掌握在自己手中。这就是我们的自由和我们坚守的信条具有的意义——这就是为何不同种族和信仰的男女老少能在此地齐聚一堂；为何有人60年前在餐馆还得不到接待，而今日他的儿子却能站在此地庄严宣誓。

为此，让我们记住这一天，记住我们是怎样的人，记住我们走过的路。在美利坚诞生的年月，在那些最寒冷的日子里，为数不多的爱国者聚集在冰河岸边，身旁的篝火即将熄灭。首都已经撤防，敌人正在进军，雪地沾满斑斑血迹。在我们的革命何去何从，结局最难以估计的时刻，美国的开国元勋向人民宣告："让我们昭告未来的世界……在这个酷寒的冬季，万物萧瑟，只有希望和美德坚忍不拔……这个城市和这个国家，受到共同危难的召唤，挺身而出，奋起迎战。"

美利坚，在我们面临共同危难之际，在我们遇到艰难险阻的冬日，让我们牢记这些永恒的话语。心怀希望和美德，让我们再一次不惧严寒，勇为中流砥柱，不论何种风暴来袭，我们必将坚不可摧。今后，让我们的子孙后代如此评说：我们在遇到考验之时没有

children that when we were tested, we refused to let this journey end, that we did not turn back, nor did we falter; and with eyes fixed on the horizon and God's grace upon us, we carried forth that great gift of freedom and delivered it safely to future generations.

半途而废，没有退缩不前，也没有丝毫动摇；让我们全神贯注，高瞻远瞩，感谢上帝对我们的恩典，继承自由这个宝贵的传统，平稳地世代相传。

单词解析 Word Analysis

instrument ['ɪnstrəmənt] *n.* 仪器；乐器；工具；器械

例 He can play nearly every musical instrument.
他几乎能演奏每一种乐器。

tolerance ['tɒlərəns] *n.* 宽容；忍耐力；容忍

例 Tolerance is another name for indifference.
宽容是不关心的别名。

patriotism ['peɪtrɪətɪzəm] *n.* 爱国主义；爱国心

例 They did evil under the veil of patriotism.
他们在爱国主义的幌子下作恶。

recognition [,rekəg'nɪʃn] *n.* 承认；认出；赏识

例 Not until 1916 did the UMW finally win recognition from the anthracite operators.
直到1916年，美国矿工联合会才终于得到无烟煤矿资方承认。

grudging ['grʌdʒɪŋ] *adj.* 吝惜的；不情愿的；勉强的

例 For as long as the world economy was growing fast, financial markets commanded grudging allegiance.
在世界经济发展迅速的时候，金融市场得到了勉强的忠诚。

citizenship ['sɪtɪzənʃɪp] *n.* 国籍；公民权；公民的身份

例 They are going to take my citizenship away.
他们打算取消我的国籍。

creed [kriːd] *n.* 宗教信仰；信念

例 People of all colors and creeds have come here to celebrate the holiday.
各种肤色和各种宗教信仰的人聚集在这里欢度节日。

sacred ['seɪkrɪd] *adj.* 神圣的；受尊重的

例 In India the cow is a sacred animal.
在印度，牛是神圣的动物。

remembrance [rɪ'membrəns] *n.* 回想；记忆；纪念品

例 The remembrance of these will add zest to his life.
回想起这些事情，使他的生活增添了乐趣。

huddle ['hʌdl] *n.* 杂乱一团；混乱；拥挤 *v.* 推挤；乱堆；草率了事

例 He shouted into the cavernous arena as if he were shouting into a huddle.
他对着球场吼叫，仿佛他面对的是混乱的人群。

语法知识点 Grammar Points

① This is the source of our confidence-the knowledge that God calls on us to shape an uncertain destiny.

这个句子中有一个结构"call on sb. to do sth."，表示"号召某人做某事"。

例 One of Kenya's leading churchmen has called on the government to resign.
肯尼亚宗教界的一位重要人物已呼吁政府下台。

② So let us mark this day with remembrance...

这个句子中有一个结构"mark sth. with sth."，表示"以……来纪念/标记……"。

例 Of course, but it's also an opportunity for players to leave their mark with eye-catching performances and mischievous quotes that invite speculation and interest about their future.
本质上的确如此，但世界杯也是球员们留下个人烙印的时候，他们用无与伦比的优异表现和恶作剧般的漫天要价引发人们对其前途的关注和兴趣。

③ ...and with eyes fixed on the horizon and God's grace upon us...

这个句子中有一个结构"fix on",表示"确定;固定;使集中于"。

例 It's difficult to fix my mind on what I'm doing.
我很难专心致志地工作。

经典名句 Famous Classics

1. You can't use up creativity. The more you use, the more you have.
   创意永远用不完,你用得越多,你拥有的创意也越多。

2. Your task is not to seek for love, but merely to seek and find all the barriers within yourself that you have built against it.
   你的任务不是寻找爱,而是寻找并发现所有你内在所建筑的不让爱进来的障碍。

3. The only impossible journey is the one you never begin.
   唯一不可能的行程,是你从未启程的那个。

4. Dreams become reality when we put our minds to it.
   如果我们全心全力,梦想将成为现实。

5. You choose the life you live. If you don't like it, it's on you to change it because no one else is going to do it for you.
   是你选择你的人生,如果你不喜欢你的人生,你得自己改变它,因为没有人会帮你改变它。

读书笔记

13 Heal the Children, Heal the World A
拯救儿童，拯救世界 A

Michael Joseph Jackson
迈克尔·约瑟夫·杰克逊（1958—2009）
2001年在牛津大学发表的演讲，倡导世界关注儿童

Thank you, thank you dear friends, from the bottom of my heart, for such a loving and spirited welcome, and thank you, Mr. President, for your kind invitation to me which I am so honored to accept. I also want to **express** a special thanks to you Shmuley. You and I have been working so hard to form Heal the Kids, and in all of our efforts you have been such a **supportive** and loving friend.

And I would also like to thank Toba Friedman, our director of operations at Heal the Kids, as well as Marilyn Piels, another central member of our Heal the Kids team. I am **humbled** to be lecturing in a place that has previously been filled by such **notable** figures as Mother Theresa, Albert Einstein, Ronald Reagan, Robert Kennedy and Malcolm X.

I suppose I should start by listing my **qualifications** to speak before you this evening. Friends, I do not claim to

衷心地感谢你们，亲爱的朋友们，谢谢你们如此热情的欢迎。尊敬的校长，对您的盛情邀请我深感荣幸。同时，我还要特别感谢犹太教教士施慕礼，您和我为了建立"拯救儿童"慈善基金会付出了艰辛的努力，并且自始至终您都是我可靠和敬爱的朋友。

我还要感谢"拯救儿童"慈善基金会的理事，我们"拯救儿童"慈善基金会团队的另一位核心成员玛丽莲·皮尔斯。在这里演讲，我感到很惭愧。因为，曾经来这里做过演讲的都是著名人士，例如，特瑞莎修女、阿尔伯特·爱因斯坦、罗纳德·里根、罗勃特·肯尼迪和马尔科姆·艾克斯。

在开始我今晚的演讲之前，我想首先说一说，为什么我有资格在此做演讲。朋友

have the academic expertise of other speakers who have addressed this hall, just as they could lay little claim at being adept at the moonwalk.

But I do have a claim to having experienced more places and cultures than most people will ever see. And friends, I have **encountered** so much in this relatively short life of mine that I still cannot believe I am only 42. I often tell Shmuley that in soul years I'm sure that I'm at least 80-and tonight I even walk like I'm 80. So please **harken** to my message, because what I have to tell you tonight can bring healing to humanity and healing to our planet.

Tonight, I come before you less as an icon of pop (whatever that means anyway), and more as an icon of a generation, a generation that no longer knows what it means to be children.

All of us are products of our childhood. But I am the product of a lack of a childhood, an absence of that precious and wondrous age when we are **frolic** playfully without a care in the world.

Those of you who are familiar with the Jackson Five know that I began performing at the tender age of five and that ever since then, I haven't stopped dancing or singing. But while performing and making music undoubtedly remain as some of my greatest joys, when I was

们，我并不具有其他来此演讲的人士所具有的学术专业知识，就像很少人能声称自己擅长"太空步"一样。

但我可以说，我游历了更多的地方，也看到了比一般人更多不同的文化。朋友们，在我相对较短暂的生命里，我经历了如此之多的事情，以至于我无法相信我只有42岁。我经常跟施慕礼说，我敢肯定我的心理年龄至少有80岁，而今晚我走路的样子更像一个80岁的老人。那么，就请大家仔细倾听我的演讲，因为今晚我所讲的内容，能治愈我们世界的人性。

今晚，我并不是以一个流行偶像的身份站在大家面前(不管那意味着什么)，而是作为一代人的标志站在这里，这是一代不知作为一个孩子意味着什么的人。

每个人都拥有过童年，但我却没有，我没有那个宝贵的和令人惊奇的年龄阶段，那时我们只需尽情玩耍，无须关心世界。

所有熟悉杰克逊五人乐队的人都知道，我不到五岁就开始表演。而且，从那以后，我就没有停止过跳舞、唱歌。尽管表演和音乐仍然是我最大的乐趣之一，但是，在我小的时

young I wanted more than anything else to be a typical little boy. I wanted to build tree houses, have water balloon fights, and play hide and seek with my friends. But fate had it otherwise and all I could do was envy the laughter and playtime that seemed to be going on all around me.

候，我还是更愿意跟其他小男孩一样，搭树屋、打水球、跟朋友一起玩捉迷藏。但是命运却事与愿违，所以我只能羡慕那些充斥在我周围的笑声和欢乐时光。

单词解析 Word Analysis

express [ɪk'spres] *v.* 表达；快递 *n.* 快车；快递
例 Jack can express himself clearly.
杰克可以清晰地表达自己。

supportive [sə'pɔːtɪv] *adj.* 支持的；支援的
例 She is extremely supportive to me.
她特别支持我。

humble ['hʌmbl] *adj.* 谦虚的
例 She excused herself with humble words.
她用谦虚的言辞为自己辩解。

notable ['nəʊtəb(ə)l] *adj.* 显著的；著名的
例 It is difficult to find out the notable difference between these two objects.
很难找出这两个物品之间的显著差别。

qualification [ˌkwɒlɪfɪ'keɪʃ(ə)n] *n.* 资格；条件
例 They had every qualification for success.
他们具备获得成功的各种条件。

encounter [ɪn'kaʊntə] *v.* 遭遇；邂逅
例 She encountered an old friend on the road.
她在路上遇到了一个老朋友。

harken ['hɑːkən] v. 倾听；留心

例 Please harken to my message attentively.
请仔细认真听我说。

frolic ['frɒlɪk] adj. 嬉戏的；欢乐的 v. 嬉戏打闹

例 A group of penguins relax and frolic on the beach.
一群企鹅在海滩上休憩打闹。

语法知识点 Grammar Points

① Thank you, thank you dear friends, from the bottom of my heart, for such a loving and spirited welcome, and thank you, Mr. President, for your kind invitation to me which I am so honored to accept.

这个句子中有一个结构"from the bottom of my heart"，表示"真心的"。

例 I would like to apologize from the bottom of my heart for causing so much trouble.
我发自内心地为自己引起的麻烦道歉。

② Friends, I do not claim to have the academic expertise of other speakers who have addressed this hall, just as they could lay little claim at being adept at the moonwalk.

这个句子中有一个结构"be adept at"，表示"擅长"。同义词组有be good at, do well in和be skilled in。

例 Barbie was adept at smiling before the camera.
芭比擅长在镜头前微笑。

③ But I am the product of a lack of a childhood, an absence of that precious and wondrous age when we are frolic playfully without a care in the world.

这个句子中有一个结构"a lack of"，表示"缺乏；缺少"。注意lack的词性为名词。Lack做动词"缺乏"讲时，直接接宾语，例如lack sth.。

例 There is a lack of fish in the river.
这条河里没什么鱼。

④ **Those of you who are familiar with the Jackson Five know that I began performing at the tender age of five.**

这个句子中有一个结构"be familiar with",表示"对……熟悉",注意区分它和be familiar to。Be familiar with主语为人;be familiar to主语为物。

例 I am familiar with this book.
This book is familiar to me.
我很熟悉这本书。

⑤ **Ever since then, I haven't stopped dancing or singing.**

这个句子中有一个结构"ever since",表示"从那时到现在"。

例 I didn't believe her ever since she cheated on me.
自从她骗我以后,我再也不相信她了。

经典名句 Famous Classics

1. Satire is a sort of glass, wherein beholders do generally discover everybody's face but their own. — Jonathan Swift
讽刺是一面镜子,观看者通常从中看到每一个人的面容却看不到自己。(斯威夫特·J.)

2. Literature is a kind of intellectual light which, like the light of the sun, may sometimes enable us to see what we do not like. — Samusel Johnson
文学是一种理智之光,它和阳光一样,有时能使我们看到我们不喜欢的东西。(约翰逊·S.)

3. When an end is lawful and obligatory, the indispensable means to it are also lawful and obligatory. — Abraham Lincoln
如果一个目的是正当而必须做的,则达到这个目的的必要手段也是正当而必须采取的。(林肯·A.)

4. Work is more that a necessary for most human beings; it is the focus of their lives, the source of their identity and creativity. — Leonard R.Sayles
对大多数人来说,工作不仅仅是一种必需,它还是人们生活的焦点,是他们的个性和创造性的源泉。(塞尔斯·L.R.)

5. We often hear of people breaking down from overwork, but in nine cases out of ten they are really suffering from worry or anxiety. —John Lubbock

我们常常听人说,人们因工作过度而垮下来,但是实际上十有八九是因为饱受担忧或焦虑的折磨。(卢伯克·J.)

读书笔记

14 Heal the Children, Heal the World B
拯救儿童，拯救世界 B

Michael Joseph Jackson
迈克尔·约瑟夫·杰克逊（1958—2009）
2001年在牛津大学发表的演讲，倡导世界关注儿童

I used to think that I was **unique** in feeling that I was without a childhood. I believed that indeed there were only a handful people with whom I could share those feelings. When I recently met with Shirley Temple Black, the great child star of the 1930s and 40s, we said nothing to each other at first. We simply cried together, for she could share a pain with me that only others like my close friends Elizabeth Taylor and McCauley Culkin knew.

I do not tell you this to gain your **sympathy** but to impress upon you my first important point —it is not just Hollywood child stars that have suffered from a nonexistent childhood. Today, it's a **universal** calamity, a global **catastrophe**. Childhood has become the great casualty of modern-day living. All around us we are producing scores of kids who have not had the joy, who have not been

我曾以为只是我自己有这种没有童年的感觉。我认为，只有极少数人可以与我一起分担那种感觉。最近，当我遇到二十世纪三四十年代的童星秀兰·邓波儿的时候，一见面我们没有说任何话，只是一起哭泣。因为她能理解我的痛苦，而这些痛苦以前只有我最亲密的朋友伊丽莎白·泰勒和麦考利·卡尔金才能体会到。

说这些并不是想博得你们的同情，只是想让你们知道我要讲的第一件重要的事情——不只是好莱坞的童星们才会遭受没有童年的痛苦。如今，它已成为一种普遍的灾难，全世界的灾难。童年已经成为了现代生活的牺牲品。我们身边有很多小孩，他们不曾拥有快乐，不曾得到应有的权利，不曾获得自由。他们甚至不知

accorded the right, who have not been allowed the freedom, or knowing what it's like to be a kid.

Today children are constantly encouraged to grow up faster, as if this period known as childhood is a burdensome stage, to be endured and ushered through, as swiftly as possible. And on that subject, I am certainly one of the world's greatest experts.

Ours is a generation that has witnessed the **abrogation** of the parent-child **covenant**. Psychologists are publishing libraries of books detailing the destructive effects of denying one's children, the unconditional love that is so necessary to the healthy development of their minds and character. And because of all the neglect, too many of our kids have, essentially, to raise themselves. They are growing more distant from their parents, grandparents and other family members, as all around us the **indestructible** bond that once glued together the generations, unravels.

This violation has bred a new generation; Generation O let us call it, which has now picked up the torch from Generation X. The O stands for a generation that has everything on the outside-wealth, success, fancy clothing and fancy cars, but an aching emptiness on the inside.

道，作为一个孩子究竟应该是怎样的。

今天，人们鼓励孩子们快点长大，好像这个被称作"童年"的时期是一个麻烦的阶段，是一个长期的需要指引的过程，越快结束越好。在这个问题上，我无疑是世界上最专业的人士之一。

我们是见证了父母与子女之间的盟约取消的一代人。心理学家们在许多书里都详细地陈述了，如果不给孩子爱会带来什么负面影响。无条件的爱对孩子们思想和性格的健康发展是十分必要的。由于人们忽视了所有这些问题，很多孩子就必须自己照顾自己。这导致他们与自己的父母、祖父母和其他家庭成员的关系越来越疏远，也导致曾经把几代人都联系在一起的、坚不可摧的凝聚力瓦解了。

这种违背常理的行为造就了新一代人，让我们称之为O时代的人，他们接过了X时代人的火炬，拥有一切外在的东西——财富、成就、精美的服装和豪车，但内心却很空虚。

我的演讲美文：神奇的时代

单词解析 Word Analysis

unique [juːˈniːk] *adj.* 独特的；稀罕的
例 We all have unique skills and gifts.
我们都有独特的技能和天赋。

sympathy [ˈsɪmpəθɪ] *n.* 同情；慰问；赞同
例 I feel sympathy for those who are involved in the war.
我对那些战争中的人表示同情。

universal [juːnɪˈvɜːsəl] *adj.* 普遍的；通用的
例 This chart will illustrate how universal these concepts are.
这个表格展示这些概念有多普遍通用。

catastrophe [kəˈtæstrəfɪ] *n.* 大灾难；大祸
例 A catastrophe is around the corner.
一场大灾难即将来临。

abrogation [ˌæbrəˈgeʃən] *n.* 废除；取消
例 The president announced the abrogation of the regulation.
主席宣布了这则条例的废除。

covenant [ˈkʌvənənt] *n.* 契约；盟约
例 Covenant in Israel becomes the basis of social ethnics.
在以色列，契约成为最基本的社会道德规范。

indestructible [ˌɪndɪˈstrʌktɪbəl] *adj.* 不可毁灭的；不能
例 He tries to convince us that the soul is immortal and indestructible.
他试图说服我们灵魂是永恒且不能毁灭的。

语法知识点 Grammar Points

① **I used to think that I was unique in feeling that I was without a childhood.**

这个句子中有一个结构"used to do"，表示"过去常常"。需要区分几个较为相似的结构be used to do，表示被用来做……；get used to doing，表示习惯于。

例 He used to play basketball when he was young.
他年轻的时候常常打篮球。
Wood is often used to make desks and chairs.
木头常常被用来制作桌椅。
He isn't used to eating Chinese food.
他不习惯吃中餐。

② **It is not just Hollywood child stars that have suffered from a nonexistent childhood.**

这个句子中有一个结构"suffer from",表示"遭受;忍受"。

例 How long have you been suffering from the headache?
你头痛有多久了?

③ **They are growing more distant from their parents, grandparents and other family members, as all around us the indestructible bond that once glued together the generations, unravels.**

这个句子中有一个结构"be distant from",表示"远离"。

例 The moon is distant from the earth.
月亮和地球距离很远。

④ **Generation O let us call it, that has now picked up the torch from Generation X.**

这个句子中有一个结构"pick up",在这里表示"捡起;拾起"。Pick up还有"接某人,通过学习或经历获得"的意思。

例 He picked up the broken pieces of glass.
他捡起了玻璃碎片。
The bus picked up three commuters at the bus stop.
公共汽车在公交站载送了三个通勤者。
I picked up French when I was in France.
我在巴黎学习了法语。

经典名句 Famous Classics

1. The office of the scholar is to cheer, to raise, and to guide men by showing them facts amidst appearances. — Ralph Waldo Emerson
   学者的工作就是通过向大众提示存在于现象中的事实来鼓舞大众、教育大众、引导大众。（爱默生·R.W.）

2. Love does not consist in gazing at each other but in looking outward together in the same direction. — Saint Exupery
   爱情不在于相互凝视，而在于共同往外朝一个方向看。（圣埃格·楚佩里）

3. Life is made up of sobs, sniffles and smiles with sniffles predominating. — O Henry
   人生是由呜咽、抽泣和微笑组成，而在三者之中，抽泣处于支配地位。（欧·亨利）

4. If you have great talents, industry will improve them; if you have but moderate abilities, industry will supply their deficiency. — Reynolds
   如果你有天赋，勤勉会使其更加完善;如果你能力一般，勤勉会补足缺陷。（雷诺兹）

5. A man is not old as long as he is seeking something. A man is not old until regrets take the place of dreams.
   只要一个人还有追求，他就没有老。直到后悔取代了梦想，一个人才算老。

读书笔记

15　Mo Yan's Nobel Prize Speech A
莫言诺贝尔文学奖演讲 A

> **Mo Yan**
> 莫言，第一个获得诺贝尔文学奖的中国籍作家
> 2012年12月8日在瑞典学院发表演讲
> 以下为演讲实录（节选），英文由Howard Goldblatt翻译

My earliest memory was taking our only **vacuum** bottle to the public canteen for drinking water. Weakened by hunger, I dropped the bottle and broke it. Scared **witless**, I hid all that day in a haystack. Toward evening, I heard my mother calling my childhood name, so I crawled out of my hiding place, prepared to receive a beating or a scolding. But Mother didn't hit me, didn't even **scold** me. She just rubbed my head and **heaved** a sigh.

My most painful memory involved going out in the collective's field with Mother to glean ears of wheat. The gleaners scattered when they spotted the watchman. But Mother, who had bound feet, could not run; she was caught and slapped so hard by the watchman, a hulk of a man, that she fell to the ground. The watchman **confiscated** the wheat we'd

我记忆中最早的一件事，是提着家里唯一的一把热水壶去公共食堂打开水。因为饥饿无力，失手将热水瓶打碎，我吓得要命，钻进草垛，一天没敢出来。傍晚时候我听到母亲呼唤我的乳名，我从草垛里钻出来，以为会受到打骂，但母亲没有打我也没有骂我，只是抚摸着我的头，口中发出长长的叹息。

我记忆中最痛苦的一件事，就是跟着母亲去集体的地里拣麦穗，看守麦田的人来了，拣麦穗的人纷纷逃跑，我母亲是小脚，跑不快，被捉住，那个身材高大的看守人扇了她一个耳光，她摇晃着身体跌倒在地，看守人没收了我们拣到的麦穗，吹着口哨扬长而去。我母亲嘴角流血，坐在地

gleaned and walked off whistling. As she sat on the ground, her lip bleeding, Mother wore a look of hopelessness I'll never forget. Years later, when I encountered the watchman, now a gray-haired old man, in the marketplace, Mother had to stop me from going up to **avenge** her. "Son," she said evenly, "the man who hit me and this man are not the same person."

My clearest memory is of a Moon Festival day, at noontime, one of those rare occasions when we ate jiaozi at home, one bowl apiece. An aging beggar came to our door while we were at the table, and when I tried to send him away with half a bowlful of dried sweet potatoes, he reacted angrily: "I'm an old man," he said. "You people are eating jiaozi, but want to feed me sweet potatoes. How heartless can you be?" I reacted just as angrily: "We're lucky if we eat jiaozi a couple of times a year, one small bowlful apiece, barely enough to get a taste! You should be thankful we're giving you sweet potatoes, and if you don't want them, you can get the hell out of here!" After (dressing me down) **reprimanding** me, Mother dumped her half bowlful of jiaozi into the old man's bowl.

上，脸上那种绝望的神情我终生难忘。多年之后，当那个看守麦田的人成为一个白发苍苍的老人，在集市上与我相逢，我冲上去想找他报仇，母亲拉住了我，平静地对我说："儿子，那个打我的人，与这个老人，并不是一个人。"

我记得最深刻的一件事是一个中秋节的中午，我们家难得的包了一顿饺子，每人只有一碗。正当我们吃饺子时，一个乞讨的老人来到了我们家门口，我端起半碗红薯干打发他，他却愤愤不平地说："我是一个老人，你们吃饺子，却让我吃红薯干。你们的心是怎么长的？"我气急败坏地说："我们一年也吃不了几次饺子，一人一小碗，连半饱都吃不了！给你红薯干就不错了，你要就要，不要就滚！"母亲训斥了我，然后端起她那半碗饺子，倒进了老人碗里。

Mo Yan's Nobel Prize Speech A
莫言诺贝尔文学奖演讲 A

单词解析 Word Analysis

vacuum ['vækjʊəm] *adj.* 真空的；空的

例 No artist works in a vacuum. They are all influenced by others.
没有艺术家是在真空中工作的。他们都是互相影响的。

witless ['wɪtlɪs] *adj.* 无知的；愚蠢的

例 This novel is centered around a witless father and his children.
这部小说主要讲述了一个愚蠢的父亲和他的孩子的故事。

scold [skəʊld] *v.* 责骂； *n.* 责骂

例 The mother scolded the child for breaking the window.
妈妈因为打破窗户而责备了孩子。

heave [hiːv] *v.* 发出（叹息）；举起 *n.* 举起；起伏

例 The doctor heaved a sigh and kept on working.
医生叹了口气，继续工作了。

confiscate ['kɒnfɪskeɪt] *v.* 没收；充公 *adj.* 被没收的

例 The policeman confiscated the robber's pistol.
警察没收了强盗的手枪。

avenge [ə'ven(d)ʒ] *v.* 报复；报仇

例 He avenged his brother.
他为兄弟报了仇。

reprimand ['reprɪmɑːnd] *v.* 谴责； *n.* 训斥

例 How do you reprimand your children when they do something wrong?
当孩子做错事的时候，你该如何训斥他们呢？

语法知识点 Grammar Points

① Toward evening, I heard my mother calling my childhood name, so I crawled out of my hiding place, prepared to receive a beating or a scolding.

这个句子中有两个结构"hear sb. doing"和"prepare to do"，分别表示"听到某人正在做某事"和"准备做某事"。

例 I heard someone singing when I passed by.
我经过的时候听到有人正在唱歌。

I'm prepared to take the exam.
我已经准备好考试了。

② **Mother had to stop me from going up to avenge her.**

这个句子中有一个结构"stop sb. from doing sth."，表示"阻止某人做某事"。同义词组有prevent sb. from doing sth.和keep sb. from doing sth.。另外注意区分它们和protect sb. from doing sth，表示保护免受伤害。

例 We must stop/keep/prevent the water from being polluted.
我们要防止水源被污染。

We must protect the children from violence.
我们要保护儿童免受暴力的伤害。

经典名句 *Famous Classics*

1. The size of your body is of little account, the size of your brain is of much account, the size of your heart is of the most account of all.
   身体的大小无关紧要，头脑的大小非常重要，而最最重要的是心灵的大小。

2. Happy are the families where the government of parents is the reign of affection, and obedience of the children the submission to love.
   幸福的家庭，父母靠慈爱当家，孩子也是出于对父母的爱而顺从大人。

3. Life being very short, and the quiet hours of it few, we ought to waste none of them on reading valueless books. — Ruskin
   生命是短暂的，生命中的宁静时刻更少，我们不应该浪费时间去读没有价值的书。（罗斯金）

4. Penitence enervates our spirit, causing a greater loss than loss itself and making a bigger mistake than mistake itself, so never regret.

后悔是一种耗费精神的情绪。后悔是比损失更大的损失，比错误更大的错误，所以不要后悔。

5. Everyone has his inherent potential which is easily concealed by habits, blured by time, and eroded by inertia.
每个人都有潜在的能量，只是很容易被习惯所掩盖、被时间所迷离、被惰性所消磨。

读书笔记

16 Mo Yan's Nobel Prize Speech B
莫言诺贝尔文学奖演讲 B

Mo Yan

莫言,第一个获得诺贝尔文学奖的中国籍作家
2012年12月8日在瑞典学院发表演讲
以下为演讲实录(节选),英文由Howard Goldblatt翻译

My most **remorseful** memory involves helping Mother sell cabbages at market, and me overcharging an old villager one jiao-**intentionally** or not, I can't **recall**-before heading off to school. When I came home that afternoon, I saw that Mother was crying, something she rarely did. Instead of scolding me, she **merely** said softly, "Son, you embarrassed your mother today."

Mother **contracted** a serious lung disease when I was still in my teens. Hunger, disease, and too much work made things extremely hard on our family. The road ahead looked especially **bleak**, and I had a bad feeling about the future, worried that Mother might take her own life. Every day, the first thing I did when I walked in the door after a day of hard labor was calling out

我最后悔的一件事,就是跟着母亲去卖白菜,有意无意地多算了一位买白菜的老人一毛钱。算完钱我就去了学校。当我放学回家时,看到很少流泪的母亲泪流满面。母亲并没有骂我,只是轻轻地说:"儿子,你让娘丢了脸。"

我十几岁时,母亲患了严重的肺病,饥饿、病痛、劳累使我们这个家庭陷入了困境,看不到光明和希望。我产生了一种强烈的不祥之兆,以为母亲随时都会自寻短见。每当我劳动归来,一进大门就高喊母亲,听到她的回应,心中才感到一块石头落了地。如果一时听不到她的回应,我就心惊胆战,跑到厨房和磨坊里寻找。有一次找遍了所有的房间也没有见到母亲的身影,我便

for Mother. Hearing her voice was like giving my heart a new **lease** on life. But not hearing her threw me into a panic. I'd go looking for her in the side building and in the mill. One day, after searching everywhere and not finding her, I sat down in the yard and cried like a baby. That is how she found me when she walked into the yard carrying a **bundle** of firewood on her back. She was very unhappy with me, but I could not tell her what I was afraid of. She knew anyway. "Son," she said, "don't worry, there may be no joy in my life, but I won't leave you till the God of the Underworld calls me."

坐在了院子里大哭。这时母亲背着一捆柴草从外面走进来。她对我的哭很不满，但我又不能对她说出我的担忧。母亲看出我的心思，她说："孩子你放心，尽管我活着没有一点乐趣，但只要阎王爷不叫我，我是不会去的。"

单词解析 Word Analysis

remorseful [rɪˈmɔːsf(ʊ)l] *adj.* 懊恼的；悔恨的

例 He knelt before his mother, bitterly remorseful.
他跪在母亲面前，悔恨交加。

intentional [ɪnˈtenʃ(ə)n(ə)l] *adj.* 故意的；蓄意的

例 He has been sent off the field for his intentional hurting.
他因故意伤人而被罚下场。

recall [rɪˈkɔːl] *v.* 回想起；召回

例 I couldn't recall what he had said at the meeting.
我想不起来他在会议上说了些什么。

merely [ˈmɪəlɪ] *adv.* 仅仅

例 I am merely reporting what he said.
我只是转述他的话。

contract ['kɒntrækt] *v.* 感染；订约 *n.* 合同
例 Unfortunately, she contracted the flu.
不幸的是，她感染了流感。

bleak [bliːk] *adj.* 阴冷的；荒凉的；黯淡的
例 The outlook for survival is bleak.
存活的希望十分渺茫。

lease [liːs] *n.* 租约 *v.* 出租
例 He leased his shop to his friends.
他将商店租给了一个朋友。

bundle ['bʌnd(ə)l] *n.* 束；捆
例 The boy presented his girlfriend a bundle of roses.
那个男孩送给他的女友一束花。

语法知识点 Grammar Points

① **Instead of scolding me, she merely said softly, "Son, you embarrassed your mother today."**

这个句子中有一个结构"instead of"，表示"代替；而不是"。

例 She spent her time in watching TV instead of studying.
她没有学习，而是把时间花费在了看电视上。

② **I had a bad feeling about the future, worried that Mother might take her own life.**

这个句子中有一个结构"take one's own life"，表示"自杀"，相当于commit suicide。

例 Although life was hard on her, she never thought about taking her own life to end the misery.
虽然生活很艰苦，但是她从来没想过以自杀来结束这痛苦。

③ **Every day, the first thing I did when I walked in the door after a day of hard labor was calling out for Mother.**

这个句子中有一个结构"call out"，表示"大声呼唤；出动"。注意call和其他介词连用的意思。call up表示打电话；call on表示号召。

例 Miners were called out on strike by union leaders.
矿工遵照工会领袖的指示举行罢工。
I'll call you up tomorrow.
我明天给你打电话。
The government called on the workers to oppose waste.
政府号召工人反对浪费。

④ **She was very unhappy with me, but I could not tell her what I was afraid of.**

这个句子中有一个结构"be afraid of",表示"害怕"。

例 Don't be afraid of loneliness.
不要害怕孤单。

经典名句 Famous Classics

1. Once we dreamt that we were strangers. We wake up to find that we were dear to each other. — Rabindranath Tagore
我们一度梦见彼此是陌生人,醒来时发现彼此是相亲相爱的。(泰戈尔)

2. I do not want people to be very agreeable, as it saves me the trouble of liking them a great deal. — Jane Austen
我不希望遇到好相处的人,因为我会很喜欢他们,喜欢别人可是件大麻烦。(简·奥斯汀)

3. A woman, especially, if she has the misfortune of knowing anything, should conceal it as well as she can. — Jane Austen
一个女人要是不幸聪明得什么都懂,那就必须同时懂得怎么伪装成什么都不懂。(简·奥斯汀)

4. A lady's imagination is very rapid; it jumps from admiration to love, from love to matrimony in a moment. — Jane Austen
女人的思维很有跳跃性:从仰慕到爱慕,从爱慕到结婚都是一眨眼间的事。(简·奥斯汀)

5. That is the thankless position of the father in the family-the provider for all, and the enemy of all.
父亲在家中处于吃力不讨好的位置——所有人的供养者,和所有人的敌人。

17 Fight for Peace A
为和平而战 A

Betty Williams
佩蒂·威廉斯1976年被授予诺贝尔和平奖
1977年12月11日在挪威首都奥斯陆市政厅发表获奖演说

I stand here today with a sense of **humility**, a sense of history, and a sense of honor. I also stand here in the name of courage to give name to a challenge.

I feel humble in officially receiving the Nobel Peace Prize, because so many people have been involved in the campaign that drew such attention to our leadership that an award like this could justifiably be made. Mairead Corrigan and I may take some satisfaction with us all the days of our lives that we did make that **initial** call, a call which unlocked the massive desire for peace within the hearts of the Northern Irish people, and as we so soon discovered, in the hearts of people around the world, not least in Norway, the **generosity** of whose people to our cause is the main reason for our current ability to expand our campaign.

But unlocking the desire for peace

今天我站在这儿，内心充满了谦卑感、历史感，以及荣誉感。我还以勇气的名义站在这里，去迎接挑战。

诺贝尔和平奖让我觉得受之有愧，因为有那么多人加入这场运动，才使得我们的行动引起了人们的广泛关注，进而才有了今天这个奖项。梅里德·科里根和我可能会因为领导了这次运动而对我们的人生倍感安慰，我们释放了隐藏在北爱尔兰人民心中对和平的强烈渴望，并很快发现了，不仅在挪威，全世界人民心里都有一份慷慨，而正是他们对这项事业的慷慨，我们才能够不断扩大运动规模。

但仅仅释放对和平的渴望是远远不够的。正如以前多次发生的情况一样，如果我们没

would never have been enough. All the energy, all the **determination** to express an **overwhelming** demand for an end to the sickening cycle of useless violence would have **reverberated** briefly and despairingly among the people, as had happened so many times before if we had not organized ourselves to use that energy and that determination positively, once and for all.

So in that first week Mairead Corrigan, Ciaran McKeown and I **founded** the Movement of the Peace People, in order to give real leadership and direction to the desire which we were certain was there, deep within the hearts of the vast majority of the people, and deep even within the hearts of those who felt, perhaps still do, feel obliged, to oppose us in public.

有积极组织起来彻底运用这种能量和决心,那么所有能量、所有希望结束那些无意义的、暴力的恶性循环的决心都会无声无息甚至渐渐消失。

因此,运动开始的第一周,我和梅里德·科里根、夏兰·麦基翁就成立了"和平人民"运动组织,以便真正引导大多数人民内心深处真实存在的渴望,甚至真正引导那些曾经、也许现在仍然公开反对我们运动的那些人的内心渴望。

单词解析 Word Analysis

humility [hjʊˈmɪlɪtɪ] *n.* 谦卑;谦逊

例 Learning requires humility.
学习需要谦逊。

initial [ɪˈnɪʃəl] *adj.* 最初的;字首的

例 Once you have agreed to the initial request, they would begin to ask for more.
一旦你同意了最初的要求,他们就会要求更多。

generosity [dʒenəˈrɒsətɪ] *n.* 慷慨;大方

我的演讲美文：神奇的时代

例 I am grateful to your generosity.
我十分感谢你的慷慨。

determination [dɪˌtɜːmɪˈneɪʃ(ə)n] *n.* 决心；果断；测定

例 What matters is determination.
重要的是要有决心。

overwhelming [ˈəʊvəˈwɛlmɪŋ] *adj.* 压倒性的；势不可挡的

例 Faced with the overwhelming task, I always turned to book for help.
当面临重要任务时，我经常向书中寻求经验帮助。

reverberate [rɪˈvɜːbəreɪt] *v.* 使回响；使反射

例 The entire valley reverberated with the sound of the temple bells.
整个山谷回荡着寺庙的钟声。

found [faʊnd] *v.* 建立

例 The committee was founded last year.
委员会是去年建立的。

语法知识点 Grammar Points

① **I stand here today with a sense of humility, a sense of history, and a sense of honor.**

这个句子中有一个结构"a sense of"，表示"……感"。A sense of humility表示谦卑感；a sense of honor表示荣誉感。

例 I have a good sense of direction.
我方向感很好。

② **I feel humble in officially receiving the Nobel Peace Prize, because so many people have been involved in the campaign that drew such attention to our leadership that an award like this could justifiably be made.**

这个句子中有两个结构"be involved in"和"draw attention to"分别表示"涉及"和"吸引对……的注意力"。

> 例 He was involved in a heated discussion.
> 他参与了一场激烈的讨论。
> She talked loudly to draw people's attention to her.
> 她大声说话为了吸引大家的注意力。

> ③ I founded the Movement of the Peace People, in order to give real leadership and direction to the desire...

这个句子中有一个结构"in order to do",表示"为了"。同义词组还有 so as to。

> 例 She arrived early in order to get a good seat.
> 她出发得很早,为了有个好座位。

> ④ ... deep within the hearts of the vast majority of the people, and deep even within the hearts of those who felt, perhaps still do, feel obliged, to oppose us in public.

这个句子中有一个结构"the majority of",表示"大部分的",相当于 most。

> 例 The majority of students have taken that course.
> 大部分学生都选了那门课程。

经典名句 Famous Classics

1. Errors, like straws, upon the surface flow; he who would search for pearls must dive below.
   错误像稻草,漂浮在水面。欲觅珍珠者,必须往水下潜。

2. Those who eat most are not always fattest; those who read most, not always wisest.
   吃得最多的人不一定最肥胖,读书最多的人不一定最聪明。

3. Three things soon pass away: the echo of the woods, the rainbow, and woman's beauty.
   三样东西最易消逝:树林的回响、彩虹和女人的美貌。

4. If you are too fortunate, you will not know yourself; if you are too unfortunate, nobody will know you.

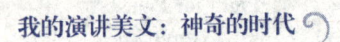

运气太好，见人不睬；运气太坏，无人理会。

5. Ordinary people merely think how they shall spend their time; a man of talent tries to use it.
   普通人只想到如何度过时间，有才能的人设法利用时间。

读书笔记

18 Fight for Peace B
为和平而战 B

Betty Williams
佩蒂·威廉斯1976年被授予诺贝尔和平奖
1977年12月11日在挪威首都奥斯陆市政厅发表获奖演说

That first week will always be remembered of course for something else besides the birth of the Peace People. For those most closely involved, the most powerful memory of that week was the death of a young republican and the deaths of three children struck by the dead man's car. A deep sense of **frustration** at the mindless **stupidity** of the continuing violence was already evident before the tragic events of that sunny afternoon of August 10, 1976. But the deaths of those four young people in one terrible moment of violence caused that frustration to explode, and create the possibility of a real peace movement.

We are for life and creation, and we are against war and destruction, and in our rage in that terrible week, we screamed that the violence had to stop.

But we also began to do something

除了成立"和平人民"运动组织，第一周当然还有其他令人难忘的事情。对于那些深入参与的人而言，最难忘的记忆就是一位年轻共和党人的离世，而且，他的车子撞死了3个小孩。这场悲剧发生于1976年8月10日，一个阳光灿烂的下午。而在此之前，人们对于此起彼伏的愚蠢的暴力事件已经表现出了明显的、深深的失望。但是在当时暴力横行的恐怖时期，4位年轻人的死亡，使人们的这种失望彻底爆发出来，并为引发一场真正的和平运动奠定了基础。

我们支持生命和创造，反对战争和破坏。在那可怕的一周，我们愤怒地喊道：必须停止暴力！

除了呐喊，我们也开始行

about it besides shouting. Ciaran McKeown wrote *The Declaration of the Peace People* which in its simple words pointed along the path of true peace, and with the **publication** of that Declaration, we announced the founding of The Movement of the Peace People, and we began planning a series of **rallies** which would last four months, and through which we would **mobilize** hundreds of thousands of people and challenge them to take the road of the Declaration.

The words are simple but the path is not easy, as all the people ever associated with the historic Nobel Peace Prize must know. It is a path on which we must not only reject the use of all the techniques of violence, but along which we must seek out the work of peace and do it. It is a way of **dedication**, hard work and courage.

Hundreds of thousands of people turned out during those four months and we would not be standing here if they had not. So I feel humble that I should be receiving this award, but I am very proud to be here in the name of all the Peace People to accept it.

动。夏兰·麦塞翁撰写了《和平人民运动宣言》，他用最朴实的语言指出了实现真正和平的道路。这一宣言发表后，我们便宣布成立和平人民运动组织，我们开始筹划持续4个月的一系列集会活动，通过集会来动员和邀请成千上万的民众一起走上和平之路。

话很简单，但这条路走起来却并不容易，历届诺贝尔和平奖获得者应该都明白这点。在这条路上，我们不仅要拒绝各种暴力手段，更要寻找和平方案并付诸实践。这是一条充满奉献、拼搏和勇气的道路。

成千上万的民众在这4个月内参与进来，如果没有他们，我们今天就不可能站在这儿。所以对于这个奖，我觉得受之有愧，但同时能在此以和平人民组织的名义领这个奖我也很自豪。

单词解析 Word Analysis

frustration [frʌˈstreɪʃn] 挫折

例 You can count on me when you are in frustration.

当你遇到挫折时，你可以依靠我。

stupidity [stʃʊ'pɪdɪtɪ] *n.* 愚蠢
- Her beauty can't make up for her stupidity.
  她的美丽不能弥补她的愚蠢。

publication [ˌpʌblɪ'keɪʃ(ə)n] *n.* 出版；出版物
- The publication of this book lifted our hopes.
  这本书的出版给我们带来了希望。

rally ['rælɪ] *n.* 集会；回复；*v.* 团结；重整
- She presided at the rally.
  她主持了这个集会。

mobilize ['məʊbəlaɪz] *v.* 动员，调动；集合
- They could now at least mobilize their armies.
  他们现在可以动员他们的军队了。

dedication [dedɪ'keɪʃ(ə)n] *n.* 奉献；献身；赠言
- This work requires patience and dedication.
  这份工作需要耐心和奉献。

语法知识点 Grammar Points

① But we also began to do something about it besides shouting.

这个句子中有一个结构"begin to do"，这个结构里的begin也可以换成start，意思是开始做某事。
- It began to snow.
  天开始下雪了。

② The words are simple but the path is not easy, as all the people ever associated with the historic Nobel Peace Prize must know.

这个句子中有一个结构"be associated with"，表示"和……联系"。
- Orange-blossom is associated with weddings.
  橙花和婚礼联系在一起。

③ **It is a path on which we must not only reject the use of all the techniques of violence, but along which we must seek out the work of peace and do it.**

这个句子中有一个结构"seek out",表示"找出;搜出"。

例 I will seek them out.
我会将他们找出来的。

④ **Hundreds of thousands of people turned out during those four months and we would not be standing here if they had not.**

这个句子中有两个结构"hundreds of thousands of"和"turn out",分别表示"无数;几十万"和"结果是;最后是"。

例 Hundreds of thousands of workers are fired each year.
每年有无数的工人被解雇。
Don't worry, everything will turn out fine.
别担心,一切都会如愿以偿的。

经典名句 Famous Classics

1. Our destiny offers not the cup of despair, but the chalice of opportunity. So let us seize it, not in fear, but in gladness.
命运给予我们的不是失望之酒,而是机会之杯。因此,让我们毫无畏惧,满心愉悦地把握命运。

2. A man can fail many times, but he isn't a failure until he begins to blame somebody else.
一个人可以失败许多次,但是只要他没有开始责怪别人,他还不是一个失败者。

3. We must accept finite disappointment, but we must never lose infinite hope. —Martin Luther King
我们必须接受失望,因为它是有限的,但千万不可失去希望,因为它是无穷的。(马丁·路德·金)

4. Make yourself a better person and know who you are before you try and know someone else and expect them to know you.
在你想了解别人也想让别人了解你之前,先完善并了解自己。

19 Save Our Planet A
拯救我们的地球 A

Steven Chu

朱棣文（1948—），美籍华人，获诺贝尔物理学奖。2009年6月4日在哈佛大学毕业典礼上发表演讲

Madame President Faust, members of the Harvard Corporation and the Board of Overseers, faculty, family, friends, and, most importantly, today's graduates, thank you for letting me share this wonderful day with you.

I am not sure I can live up to the high **standards** of Harvard Commencement speakers. Last year, J·K Rowling, the billionaire novelist, who started as a classics student, graced this **podium**. The year before, Bill Gates, the mega-billionaire **philanthropist** and computer nerd, stood here. Today, sadly, you have me. I am not a billionaire, but at least I am a nerd.

I am grateful to receive an **honorary** degree from Harvard, an honor that means more to me than you might imagine. You may have heard this morning that I was the academic failure

尊敬的福斯特校长，哈佛集团和监管理事会的各位成员，全体教员、各位家长、各位朋友，还有最重要的——今天的毕业生们，谢谢让我与你们一起分享这美好的一天。

我不太确定自己是否够得上在哈佛大学毕业典礼上演讲的水平。去年，站在这里的是亿万富翁的小说家J.K.罗琳，而她曾是一个古典文学的学生。而前年站在这里的则是超级亿万富翁、慈善家、计算机天才比尔·盖茨。今天，很遗憾，给你们演讲的人是我。我并不是一个亿万富翁，但至少我也算一个高手吧。

我很感谢哈佛大学能授予我这个荣誉学位。这对我很重要，也许比你们想象的还要重要。今天早晨你们应该已经听

of my family. Both of my brothers have degrees from Harvard. My older brother, Gilbert, has an M.D.-Ph.D. from Harvard. My younger brother, Morgan, who was just named today to the Board of Overseers, has a law degree. I was awarded a Nobel Prize. I thought my mother would be pleased. Not so. When I called her on the morning of the **announcement**, she replied, "That's nice, but when are you going to visit me next." Now, as the last brother with a degree from Harvard, maybe, at last, she will be satisfied.

Another difficulty with giving a Harvard **commencement** address is that some students may disapprove of the fact that I am borrowing material from my previous speeches and from other authors. I ask that you forgive me for two reasons.

First, in order to be heard, it is important to deliver the same message more than once. it is important to be the first person to make a discovery, but it is even more important to be the last person to make that discovery.

Second, authors who borrow from others are following in the footsteps of the best. Ralph Waldo Emerson, who graduated from Harvard at the age of 18, noted "All my best thoughts were stolen by the ancients." Picasso **declared**

说，在学术上我是我们家的失败者。我的两个兄弟都获得了哈佛大学的学位。我的哥哥，吉伯特，拥有哈佛大学医学、哲学双博士学位。我的弟弟，摩根，今天刚刚被提名为监管理事会的一员，他拥有哈佛大学的法律学位。当我被授予诺贝尔奖的时候，我就想我的母亲应该会非常高兴。但事实并非如此。得到消息那天，我给她打电话，她说："挺好的，但是我想知道你下次什么时候来看我？"也许这一次，作为在兄弟当中最后一个拿到了哈佛学位的我，她会感到满意吧。

在哈佛大学毕业典礼上作演讲的另一个难处是：有些同学可能会不喜欢我借鉴自己以前的演讲和其他人演讲中的内容。对此，我有两个理由，希望你们能给予原谅。

首先，为了让大家能理解我说的话，重复传达信息是很重要的。在科学中，第一个发现者是重要的，但是在得到公认前，最后一个做出这个发现的人也许更重要。

其次，借鉴他人的创作者，其实是在追随那些最优秀的人的脚步。拉尔夫·沃尔多·爱默生，18岁毕业于哈佛大学，他曾写下："我最好的思

"Good artists borrow. Great artists steal." Why should commencement speakers be held to a higher standard?

毕加索也曾宣称:"优秀的艺术家借鉴,伟大的艺术家偷窃。"那么,为什么毕业典礼演说者就不持同样的标准呢?

单词解析 Word Analysis

standard ['stændəd] *n.* 标准

例 He insisted on a high academic standard.
他坚持要求高的学术标准。

podium ['pəʊdɪəm] *n.* 领奖台

例 It would be great if we all made the podium.
如果我们都登上领奖台就太好了。

philanthropist [fɪˈlænθrəpɪst] *n.* 慈善家

例 Bill Gates is a philanthropist.
比尔·盖茨是个慈善家。

honorary [ˈɒn(ə)(rə)rɪ] *adj.* 荣誉的;名誉的

例 She got her honorary degree at Peking University.
她在北京大学获得了名誉学位。

announcement [əˈnaʊnsm(ə)nt] *n.* 公告;宣告

例 They began to shoot after the announcement.
他们在发布通告后开始射击。

commencement [kəˈmensm(ə)nt] *n.* 毕业典礼;开始;发端

例 The commencement was held in the grand hall.
毕业典礼在礼堂举行。

declare [dɪˈkleə] *v.* 宣布;声明

例 He declared his love to her.
他向她表明了爱意。

语法知识点 Grammar Points

① **Thank you for letting me share this wonderful day with you.**

这个句子中有一个结构"thank sb. for doing sth.",表示"感谢某人做某事"。

例 Thank you for inviting me to your school.
感谢邀请我来你们的学校。

② **I am not sure I can live up to the high standards of Harvard Commencement speakers.**

这个句子中有一个结构"live up to",表示"不辜负"。

例 He lived up to his promise.
他没有辜负自己的诺言。

③ **I am grateful to receive an honorary degree from Harvard, an honor that means more to me than you might imagine. You may have heard this morning that I was the academic failure of my family.**

这个句子中有一个结构"be grateful to",表示"感激;感谢"。

例 He was grateful to his teacher.
他很感激他的老师。

④ **Another difficulty with giving a Harvard commencement address is that some students may disapprove of the fact that I am borrowing material from my previous speeches and from other authors.**

这个句子中有两个结构"disapprove of"和"the fact that",分别表示"不赞成"和"……的事实",后者that引导了一个fact的同位语从句。

例 The teacher disapproved of what he had said in the class.
老师对于他在课堂上的言论十分不赞成。

We had to admit the fact that we failed in the exam.
我们不得不承认我们考试没有及格。

经典名句 Famous Classics

1. Human felicity is produced not so much by great pieces of good fortune that seldom happen, as by little advantages that occur every day.
   与其说人类的幸福来自偶尔发生的鸿运，不如说来自每天都有的小实惠。

2. The secret of being miserable is to have leisure to bother about whether you are happy or not.
   痛苦的奥秘在于有闲工夫担心自己是否幸福。

3. Happiness lies not in the mere possession of money; it lies in the joy of achievement, in the thrill of creative effort.
   幸福不在于拥有金钱，而在于获得成就时的喜悦以及产生创造力的激情。

4. Ideal is the beacon. Without ideal, there is no secure direction; without direction, there is no life.
   理想是指路明灯。没有理想，就没有坚定的方向；没有方向，就没有生活。

5. Histories make men wise; poems witty; the mathematics subtle; natural philosophy deep; moral grave; logic and rhetoric able to contend.
   历史使人明智；诗词使人灵秀；数学使人周密；自然哲学使人深刻；伦理使人庄重；逻辑修辞学使人善辩。

读书笔记

20 Save Our Planet B
拯救我们的地球 B

Steven Chu
朱棣文（1948年2月28日—），美籍华人，获诺贝尔物理学奖。2009年6月4日在哈佛大学毕业典礼上发表演讲

My address will follow the classical sonata form of commencement addresses. The first movement, just presented, was light-hearted remarks. This next movement consists of **unsolicited** advice, which is rarely valued, seldom remembered, never followed. As Oscar Wilde said, "The only thing to do with good advice is to pass it on. It is never of any use to oneself."

Here comes the advice.

First, every time you celebrate an achievement, be thankful to those who made it possible. Thank your parents and friends who supported you, thank your professors who were **inspirational**, and especially thank the other professors whose less-than-brilliant lectures forced you to teach yourself. Going forward, the ability to teach yourself is the

毕业典礼演讲都遵循古典奏鸣曲的结构，我的演讲也不例外。刚才是第一乐章——轻快的闲谈。接下来的第二乐章是送上门的忠告。这样的忠告很少有价值，几乎注定被忘记，永远不会被实践。正如奥斯卡·王尔德所说："对于忠告，我们唯一能做的就是把它传递下去。因为它对我们自身没有丝毫的用处。"

下面就是我的忠告。

首先，每一次当你庆祝取得的成就时，要感激那些助你成功的人。要感谢支持你的父母和朋友；感谢点拨你的教授；尤其要感谢那些课上得不好的教授们，正是他们的课迫使你去自学。展望未来，自学能力将会是优秀的文科教育的主要特征，也将是你成功的关

hallmark of a great liberal arts education and will be the key to your success. To your fellow students who have added immeasurably to your education during those late night discussions, hug them.

Second, in your future life, **cultivate** a generous spirit. In all **negotiations**, don't bargain for the last, little advantage. Leave the change on the table. In your **collaborations**, always remember that "credit" is not a conserved quantity. In a successful collaboration, everybody gets 90% of the credit.

Jimmy Stewart, as Elwood P. Dowd in the movie *Harvey*, got it exactly right. "Years ago my mother used to say to me, 'in this world, Elwood, you must be...she always used to call me Elwood...in this world, Elwood, you must be so smart, or so pleasant. Well, for years I was smart...I recommend pleasant. You may quote me."

Advice is as follows. As you begin this new stage of your lives, you don't have a passion, don't be satisfied until you find one. Life is too short to go through it without caring deeply about something. When I was your age, I was incredibly single-minded in my goal to be a physicist. After college, I spent eight years as a graduate student and post doc at Berkeley, and then nine years at Bell Labs. During that time, my

键。你还要对你的同学们表示谢意，他们陪伴你到深夜，对你给予无限帮助，因此，拥抱他们吧！

其次，在未来的生活中，做一个慷慨大方的人。在任何的谈判中都不要为最后一点点利益斤斤计较。给对方留一点利益的余地。在合作中，不要把荣誉留给自己。成功合作的任何一方，都应获得全部荣誉的90%。

在电影《哈维》中，吉米·斯图尔特扮演的埃尔伍德·多德，就完全理解这一点。"多年前我的母亲经常对我说'埃尔伍德，活在这个世界上，你要……她过去常常叫我埃尔伍德……活在这个世界上，你要么做一个聪明人，要么做一个好人'。这么多年来，我都做了一个聪明人……但我建议你们做个好人。你们可以引用我的这句话。"

我的第三条建议是：当你们开始人生新的阶段时，请追随你的爱好。如果你没有爱好，那就去寻找吧，在找到之前千万不能满足。生命太短暂，所以不能空手走过，你必须对某样东西倾注你的深情。我在你们这个年龄，是超级的一根筋，我的目标就是非成为物理学家不可。本科毕业后，

central focus and professional joy was physics.

Here is my final advice. Pursuing a personal passion is important, but it should not be your only goal. When you are old and gray, and look back on your life, you will want to be proud of what you have done. The source of that pride won't be the things you have acquired or the **recognition** you have received. It will be the lives you have touched and the difference you have made.

我在加州大学伯克利分校又待了8年，读完了研究生，做完了博士后，然后去贝尔实验室待了9年。在这些年中，我关注的中心和职业上的全部乐趣，都来自物理学。

我还有最后一个忠告：追求个人爱好固然很重要，但是它不是你唯一的目标。当你白发苍苍、垂垂老矣回首人生时，你需要为自己做过的事感到自豪。物质生活和你实现的占有欲，都不会产生自豪。只有那些受你影响、被你改变过的人和事，才会让你产生自豪。

单词解析 Word Analysis

unsolicited [ˌʌnsəˈlɪsɪtɪd] *adj.* 未经请求的；主动提供的

例 She's always full of unsolicited advice.
她总是未经请求就提供好多建议。

inspirational [ˌɪnspɪˈreɪʃ(ə)n(ə)l] *adj.* 鼓舞人心的；带有灵感的

例 Gandhi was an inspirational figure.
甘地是一位有号召力的人物。

cultivate [ˈkʌltɪveɪt] *v.* 培养

例 How do we cultivate positive attitudes?
我们该如何培养积极的态度呢？

negotiation [nɪˌɡəʊʃɪˈeɪʃ(ə)n] *n.* 谈判

例 The negotiation leads nowhere.
这次谈判无果。

collaboration [kəˌlæbəˈreɪʃn] *n.* 合作；协作

例 There is great opportunity for collaboration.
合作的机遇是巨大的。

recognition [rekəg'nɪʃ(ə)n] *n.* 识别；承认；重视；认出
例 The scientist deserves recognition for his talent.
这名科学家的才华应受到承认。

语法知识点 Grammar Points

① **This next movement consists of unsolicited advice, which is rarely valued, seldom remembered, never followed.**

这个句子中有一个结构"consist of"，表示"包括"。同义词组有be made up of和be constitutive of。

例 Each group shall consist of ten students.
每个组应该包括十个学生。

② **The only thing to do with good advice is to pass it on. It is never of any use to oneself.**

这个句子中有两个结构"pass on"和"of use"，分别表示"传递；继续"和"有用"。其中"of +名词"相当于对应的形容词，例如of use 等于useful；of importance等于important。

例 This ring has been passed on in my family from my mother to daughter.
在我家里，这个戒指是妈妈留给女儿的。
This book is of great use to the English learning.
这本书对于英语学习十分有帮助。

③ **The ability to teach yourself is the hallmark of a great liberal arts education and will be the key to your success.**

这个句子中有一个结构"the key to"，表示"……的答案；……的关键"，要注意介词"to"的使用。

例 The key to the success is patience and dedication.
成功的关键是耐心和决心。

④ **It will be the lives you have touched and the difference you have made.**

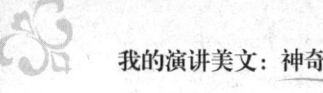

这个句子中有一个结构"make the difference",表示"关系重大;有所作为"。

例 Attitude decides everything; details make the difference.
态度决定一切;细节决定成败。

经典名句 Famous Classics

1. Don't part with your illusions. When they are gone you may still exist, but you have ceased to live.
   不要放弃你的幻想。当幻想没有了以后,你还可以生存,但是你虽生犹死。

2. The people who get on in this world are the people who get up and look for circumstances they want, and if they cannot find them, they make them.
   在这个世界上,取得成功的人是那些努力寻找他们想要机会的人,如果找不到机会,他们就去创造机会。

3. If you're walking down the right path and you're willing to keep walking, eventually you'll make progress.
   如果你走的道路正确,并坚持走下去,最终你会成功的。

4. Man might think that few women fit him before his marriage, and contrarily when they get married.
   男人在结婚前觉得适合自己的女人太少,结婚后觉得适合自己的女人很多。

5. Everyone has his inherent ability which is easily concealed by habits, blurred by time, and eroded by laziness.
   每个人都有潜能,只是很容易被习惯所掩盖,被时间所迷离,被惰性所消磨。

21 To Build an Effective Multilateral System A
建立有效的多边关系 A

Kofi Atta Annan
科菲·阿塔·安南（1938—2018）
2006年12月11日，安南在位于美国密苏里州独立市的杜鲁门总统图书馆发表告别致辞

Thank you, Senator Hagel for that wonderful **introduction**. It is a great honor to be introduced by such a **distinguished** legislator. And thanks to you, Mr. Devine, and all your staff, and to the wonderful UNA chapter of Kansas City, for all you have done to make this occasion possible.

What a pleasure and a **privilege** to be here in Missouri. It's almost a homecoming for me. Nearly half a century ago I was a student about 400 miles north of here, in Minnesota. I arrived there straight from Africa-and I can tell you, Minnesota soon taught me the value of a thick overcoat, a warm scarf...and even ear-muffs!

When you leave one home for another, there are always lessons to be learnt. And I had more to learn when I moved on from Minnesota to the United

感谢哈格尔议员精彩的介绍。能由这样一位杰出的立法委员做介绍我深感荣幸。谢谢迪瓦恩先生和你的所有员工，谢谢堪萨斯城的联合国协会分会，正因为有了你们的努力，才有了现在的这个盛会。

能够来到密苏里州，我感到十分喜悦和荣幸。对我来说就像是回家一样。大约在50年前，我在这里以北400英里的明尼苏达州上学。我是从非洲直接去那里的。我告诉你们，明尼苏达州很快让我明白了一件厚外套、一条温暖的围巾还有一副耳罩有多重要。

当从一个家走向另一个家时，你总是会有很多东西要学习。当我从明尼苏达州来到联合国要学习的东西就更多了。联合国是我们整个人类不

Nations-the **indispensable** common house of the entire human family, which has been my main home for the last 44 years. Today I want to talk particularly about five lessons I have learnt in the last ten years, during which I have had the difficult but **exhilarating** role of Secretary-General.

I think it's especially fitting that I do that here in the house that honors the legacy of Harry S Truman. If FDR was the architect of the United Nations, President Truman was the master-builder and the faithful champion of the Organization in its first years, when it had to face quite different problems from the ones FDR had expected. Truman's name will forever be associated with the memory of far-sighted American leadership in a great global **endeavor** and you will see that every one of my five lessons brings me to the conclusion that such leadership is no less sorely needed now than it was sixty years ago.

My first lesson is that, in today's world, the security of every one of us is linked to that of everyone else.

That was already true in Truman's time.

But how much more true it is in our open world today: a world where SARS, or avian flu, can be carried across oceans, let alone national borders, in a matter of

可缺少的共同家园，在过去的44年，这里一直是我的家。今天我尤其想谈谈在过去的十年里学到的五个教训，在这十年里，我担任着联合国秘书长一职，这是一个困难重重却又令人激动的职位。

我想在这个纪念哈里·杜鲁门的地方发表这个演说十分合适。如果罗斯福总统是联合国的缔造者，那么杜鲁门总统就是联合国初期主要的建设者和忠实的拥护者，当时联合国面临的问题与罗斯福总统所预料到的问题大不相同。杜鲁门的名字及他在为全球努力的过程中展现出的具有远见卓识的领导能力将一起被人们所铭记。你们将会看到，我的五个教训中的每一个教训都让我得出这样一个结论：现在这样的领导能力和六十年前一样是极度需要的。

我的第一个教训就是，在当今世界，我们每一个人的安全和其他人的安全都是紧密相连的。

在杜鲁门时代就是如此。

在今天这个开放的世界更是如此：在这个世界里，非典或禽流感在几个小时之内就可以跨越大洋进行传播，更不用说跨越国界了；气候改变的方

To Build an Effective Multilateral System A
建立有效的多边关系 A

hours; a world where even the climate is changing in ways that will affect the lives of everyone on the planet.

式将会影响这个星球上每一个人的生活。

单词解析 Word Analysis

introduction [ˌɪntrəˈdʌkʃ(ə)n] *n.* 介绍；引进；采用

例 Can you give us a brief introduction?
你能给我们做一个简要介绍吗？

distinguished [dɪˈstɪŋgwɪʃt] *adj.* 著名的；卓著的

例 Let's welcome the distinguished guests to our school.
让我们欢迎尊贵的嘉宾来我校。

privilege [ˈprɪvəlɪdʒ] *n.* 特权；优待

例 Who gave you the privilege to open the door?
是谁给你特权开门的？

indispensable [ˌɪndɪˈspensəb(ə)l] *adj.* 不可缺少的；绝对重要的

例 Dictionaries are indispensable in English study.
词典对于英语学习来说是必不可少的。

exhilarating [ɪgˈzɪləreɪtɪŋ] *adj.* 使人愉快的；令人喜欢的

例 It is exhilarating to do what we love.
可以做自己喜欢做的事情是令人愉快欢喜的。

endeavor [ɪnˈdevə] *n.* 努力；尽力 *v.* 努力；尽力

例 They made every endeavor to find the answer.
他们努力找寻答案。

语法知识点 Grammar Points

① And thanks to you, Mr. Devine, and all your staff, and to the wonderful UNA chapter of Kansas City, for all you have done to make this occasion possible.

这个句子中有一个结构"thanks to",表示"幸亏"。

例 Thanks to your help, we could finish the task in time.
多亏了你的帮助,我们才能及时地完成任务。

② **Truman's name will forever be associated with the memory of far-sighted American leadership...**

这个句子中有一个结构"be associated with",表示"和……联系;与……有关"。

例 I haven't been associated with this man for over a year.
我已经有一年多没有和这个男人联系了。

③ **My first lesson is that, in today's world, the security of every one of us is linked to that of everyone else.**

这个句子中有一个结构"be linked to",表示"与……连接;与……有关联"。

例 The pay will be linked to the inflation rate.
将工资的增长与通货膨胀率的上升挂钩。

④ **A world where SARS, or avian flu, can be carried across oceans, let alone national borders, in a matter of hours;**

这个句子中有一个结构"let alone",表示"更不必说;不打扰"。

例 Let him alone. He needs a rest.
别打扰他,他需要休息一下。

经典名句 Famous Classics

1. The future belongs to those who believe in the beauty of their dreams.
未来属于那些相信梦想之美好的人。

2. Always go with the choice that scares you the most, because that's the one that is going to require the most from you.
就做那个让你最不安的事情,因为它能发挥你最大的潜能。

3. Every day may not be good, but there's something good in every day.

不见得每天都是好日子，但是每天总会有些好事发生的。

4. The minute you think of giving up, think of the reason why you held on so long.
在你想要放弃的那一刻，想想为什么当初坚持走到了这里。

5. I think the best attitude toward life is to keep your humor on and show your smile to what happens.
人生在世，八方风雨；不妨一笑，淡然处之。

读书笔记

22 To Build an Effective Multilateral System B
建立有效的多边关系 B

Kofi Atta Annan
科菲·阿塔·安南（1938—2018）
2006年12月11日，安南在位于美国密苏里州独立市的杜鲁门总统图书馆发表告别致辞

Against such **threats** as these, no nation can make itself secure by seeking **supremacy** over all others. We all share responsibility for each other's security, and only by working to make each other secure can we hope to achieve lasting security for ourselves.

And I would add that this responsibility is not simply a matter of states being ready to come to each other's aid when attacked-important though that is. It also includes our shared responsibility to protect populations from **genocide**, war crimes, **ethnic** cleansing and crimes against **humanity**-a responsibility solemnly accepted by all nations at last year's UN summit. That means that respect for national **sovereignty** can no longer be used as a shield by governments' intent on massacring their own people,

面对这些威胁，任何国家都不能通过追求对其他国家的优势来保障自己国家的安全。我们对彼此的安全承担着责任，只有努力保障彼此的安全，我们才有希望达到我们自己持久的安全。

我还想说这个责任不仅仅是国家准备好在受到攻击时互相帮助——尽管这一点很重要。它还包括我们共同的责任来保护人们不受到种族灭绝、战争、种族清洗和反人类罪的威胁——在去年的联合国峰会上所有的国家都庄重地接受了这个责任。那就意味着尊重国家主权不能再作为政府意图对自己人民进行大屠杀的盾牌，或者是作为我们其他人在发生如此滔天罪恶时却无动于衷的借口。

or as an excuse for the rest of us to do nothing when such **heinous** crimes are committed.

But, as Truman said, "If we should pay merely lip service to inspiring ideals, and later do violence to simple justice, we would draw down upon us the bitter wrath of generations yet unborn." And when I look at the murder, rape and starvation to which the people of Darfur are being subjected, I fear that we have not gone far beyond "lip service". The lesson here is that high-sounding doctrines like the "responsibility to protect" will remain pure rhetoric unless and until those with the power to intervene effectively-by **exerting** political, economic or, in the last resort, military muscle-are prepared to take the lead.

And I believe we have a responsibility not only to our contemporaries but also to future generations-a responsibility to preserve resources that belong to them as well as to us, and without which none of us can survive. That means we must do much more, and urgently, to prevent or slow down climate change. Every day that we do nothing, or too little, imposes higher costs on our children and our children's children.

然而，正如杜鲁门所说："如果我们只是在口头上说说那些鼓舞人心的理想，然后对简单公正施以暴力，那么我们会招来未出生的后代们的强烈愤恨。"当我看到达尔富尔人民所遭遇的谋杀、强奸和饥饿问题，我害怕我们离"口头上说说"并不远。这里的教训是，诸如"保护的责任"等夸夸其谈的说法只是华丽虚饰的语言，除非那些有力量做出有效干预的国家——运用政治、经济或者不得已的时候采用军事手段——准备好起带头作用。

并且，我认为我们不仅对同代的人负有一份责任，对后代也负有一份责任——保护属于他们也是属于我们的资源，没有这些资源，我们没有人能够存活下去。那就意味着我们必须要做更多的事情，首先要阻止和减慢气候变化，这很紧迫。我们每天什么都不做或者做得太少，就会让我们的子孙后代付出更大的代价。

单词解析 Word Analysis

threat [θret] *n.* 威胁；恐吓

例 He broke her by the threat of blackmail.
他用敲诈勒索的威胁使她屈服。

supremacy [s(j)uːˈpreməsɪ] *n.* 霸权；至高无上；主权

例 The company challenged the supremacy of the current government.
这家公司质疑了现今政府的权威。

genocide [ˈdʒenəsaɪd] *n.* 种族灭绝

例 He was the victim of genocide.
他是种族灭绝的受害者。

ethnic [ˈeθnɪk] *adj.* 种族的；民族的

例 The school teaches pupils from different ethnic group.
这个学校教来自各个民族的学生。

humanity [hjʊˈmænɪtɪ] *n.* 人类；人性；人文学科

例 This crime is against humanity.
这项罪行是反人类的。

sovereignty [ˈsɒvrɪntɪ] *n.* 主权；主权国家

例 This is critical for the sovereignty of Iraq and Afghanistan.
这对于伊拉克和阿富汗的主权是至关重要的。

heinous [ˈhiːnəs] *adj.* 可憎的；凶恶的

例 It is a heinous act against human right.
这种可憎的行为侵犯了人权。

exert [ɪgˈzɜːt] *v.* 运用；发挥

例 We must exert ourselves to catch up with them.
我们必须奋力追赶他们。

To Build an Effective Multilateral System B
建立有效的多边关系 B

语法知识点 *Grammar Points*

① **Only by working to make each other secure can we hope to achieve lasting security for ourselves.**

这个句子中有一个结构"only +状语位于句首时，其后习惯于用部分倒装"，表示"只有这样才能……"，其中only后的状语可以是副词、介词短语、从句等。

例 Only in this way can we learn English well.
   只有这样才能学好英语。

② **And I believe we have a responsibility not only to our contemporaries but also to future generations-a responsibility to preserve resources that belong to them as well as to us, and without which none of us can survive.**

这个句子中有两个结构"not only...but also..."和"belong to"，分别表示"不但……而且……"和"属于"。其中"not only...but also..."后面要注意主谓一致，遵从就近原则。

例 Not only you but also I am a teacher.
   不仅是你还有我也是一名老师。
   The book belongs to him.
   这本书是他的。

③ **That means we must do much more, and urgently, to prevent or slow down climate change.**

这个句子中有一个结构"slow down"，表示"减速；放慢速度"。反义词组是speed up。

例 The car slowed down when it passed the Customs.
   过海关的时候车减慢了速度。

④ **Every day that we do nothing, or too little, imposes higher costs on our children and our children's children.**

这个句子中有一个结构"impose on"，表示"利用；欺骗；施加影响于"。

例 He always imposes his opinions on others.
   他总是把自己的意见强加于人。

107

经典名句 Famous Classics

1. When you're down and out, remember to keep your head up. When you're up and well, remember to keep your feet down.
   穷困潦倒时,要抬头挺胸;春风得意时,要脚踏实地。

2. When work is a pleasure, life is joy! When work is duty, life is slavery. — Maxime Gorki
   工作是一种乐趣时,生活是一种享受!工作是一种义务时,生活则是一种苦役。(马克西姆·高尔基)

3. Life is more like a battlefield. If you want something, you have to fight your best for it.
   生活就好比一个战场,如果你想得到一样东西,就必须拼命去争取。

4. Forget all the reason why it won't work and believe the one reason why it will.
   忘掉所有那些"不可能"的借口,去坚持那一个"可能"。

读书笔记

23 Stay Hungry, Stay Foolish A
求知若饥，虚心若愚 A

Steve Jobs
史蒂夫·乔布斯2005年在斯坦福大学毕业典礼上的著名演讲

Thank you.

I'm honored to be with you today for your **commencement** from one of the finest **universities** in the world. Truth be told, I never graduated from college, and this is the closest I've ever gotten to a college graduation. Today, I want to tell you three stories from my life. That's it. No big deal. Just three stories.

The first story is about connecting the dots. I dropped out of Reed College after the first six months, but then stayed around as a drop-in for another 18 months or so before I really quit. So why did I drop out?

It started before I was born. My **biological** mother was a young, **unwed** graduate student, and she decided to put me up for adoption. She felt very strongly that I should be **adopt**ed by college graduates, so everything was all set for me to be adopted at birth by a lawyer and his wife-except that when I popped out they decided at the last

谢谢大家。

今天，有幸见证各位从世界上最好的学校之一毕业。我从来没从大学毕业。说实话，这是我离大学毕业最近的一刻。今天，我只说三个故事，不谈大道理，只讲三个故事。

第一个故事，关于串起人生中的点点滴滴。我在里德学院待了6个月就休学了。但之后仍作为旁听生混了18个月后才最终离开。那么，我为什么休学呢？

这得从我出生之前讲起。我的亲生母亲当时是一位在读研究生，一名年轻的未婚妈妈，于是她决定把我送给别人收养。她坚持认为我应该被一对念过大学的夫妇收养，所以在我出生时，她就做好了让一位律师和他太太收养我的所有准备。但在最后一刻，这对夫妇反悔了，他们想收养一个女孩。

minute that they really wanted a girl.

So my parents, who were on a waiting list, got a call in the middle of the night asking, "We've got an unexpected baby boy; do you want him?" They said, "Of course." My biological mother found out later that my mother had never graduated from college and that my father had never graduated from high school. She refused to **sign** the final adoption papers. She only **relented** a few months later when my parents promised that I would go to college. This was the start in my life.

And 17 years later I did go to college. But I **naively** chose a college that was almost as expensive as Stanford, and all of my working-class parents' savings were being spent on my college **tuition**. After six months, I couldn't see the value in it. I had no idea what I wanted to do with my life and no idea how college was going to help me figure it out. And here I was spending all of the money my parents had saved their entire life.

So I decided to **drop** out and trust that it would all work out okay. It was pretty scary at the time, but looking back it was one of the best decisions I ever made. The minute I dropped out I could stop taking the required classes that didn't interest me, and begin dropping in on the ones that looked far more interesting.

所以在收养名单上的另一对夫妻——我的养父母——在一天半夜里接到一个电话，问他们"有一位不请自来的男婴，你们想要收养他吗？"而他们的回答是"当然要"。然而后来，我的生母发现，我的养母并未大学毕业，我的养父甚至连高中都没毕业。她拒绝在最后的收养文件上签名。直到几个月后，我的养父母保证将来一定会送我上大学，她的态度才有所转变。这便是我人生的开始。

十七年后，我上大学了。但因年幼无知，我选了一所几乎跟斯坦福一样昂贵的大学，我的父母都是工人阶级，他们倾其所有资助我的学业。六个月后，我看不出念大学的价值何在。那时候，我不知道这辈子要干什么，也不知道念大学能对我有什么帮助，而且我为了念大学，花光了我父母这辈子的所有积蓄。

所以我决定退学，相信船到桥头自然直。当时这个决定看来相当可怕，可是现在看来，那是我这辈子做过最好的决定之一。从我退学那一刻起，我再也不用上我没兴趣的必修课，而是可以去听那些我感兴趣的课。

单词解析 *Word Analysis*

commencement [kə'mensmənt] *n.* 开始；毕业典礼

例 Seeds begin to burgeon at the commencement of spring.
春天来临时种子开始发芽。

university [ˌjuːnɪ'vɜːsəti] *n.* 大学

例 John is one of his alumni in the university.
约翰是他大学时的校友之一。

biological [ˌbaɪə'lɒdʒɪkl] *adj.* 生物的；生物学的

例 The school has a large biological laboratory.
这所学校有一个很大的生物实验室。

unwed [ʌn'wed] *adj.* 未婚的

例 The unwed mother is distraught.
这名未婚妈妈精神错乱。

adopt [ə'dɒpt] *v.* 采用；收养；接受

例 They adopt new techniques in raising sheep.
他们采用新的养羊技术。

sign [saɪn] *n.* 手势；招牌；符号；迹象；正负号 *v.* 签；签名；做手势；做标记

例 I talked with him by signs.
我和他用手势交谈。

relent [rɪ'lent] *v.* 变宽厚；变温和；动怜悯之心；缓和；（坏天气）变好

例 At first she threatened to dismiss us all, but later she relented.
起初她威胁要解雇我们所有的人，但是后来她态度软化了。

naively [naɪ'iːvli] *adv.* 天真地

例 They naively assume things can only get better.
他们天真地以为情况只会变好。

tuition [tju'ɪʃn] *n.* 学费；教诲；教学

例 The money is sufficient to cover the tuition.

111

这笔钱够付学费。

drop [drɒp] *v.* 落下；跌倒；下降；放弃；漏掉；断绝关系 *n.* 滴；微量；减少；滴状物

例 She dropped to safety from the burning building.
她从失火的建筑物上坠落到安全的地方。

语法知识点 Grammar Points

① **Truth be told, I never graduated from college, and this is the closest I've ever gotten to a college graduation.**

这个句子中有一个结构"graduate from"，表示"从……毕业"。

例 She graduated from an American college.
她从一所美国的学院毕业。

② **I dropped out of Reed College after the first six months...**

这个句子中有一个结构"drop out of"，表示"从……退学，退出，退去"。

例 Some delegates walked out in a show of protest.
有几位代表退出会场以示抗议。

③ **...except that when I popped out they decided at the last minute that they really wanted a girl.**

这个句子中有一个结构"pop out"，表示"突然出现，突出"。

例 His eyes almost popped out in surprise.
他惊讶得眼睛快掉出来了。

经典名句 Famous Classics

1. Leadership is practiced not so much in words as in attitude and in actions.
领导不是通过言语，而是通过态度及行动。

2. Nothing, I am sure, calls forth the faculties so much as the being obliged to struggle with the world.

我确定，比起被迫与世界挣扎，没有什么更能唤醒我们的能力。

3. The man who has confidence in himself gains the confidence of others.
   对自己有信心的人，也可以获得别人对他的信心。

4. Only by self-respect will you compel others to respect you.
   只有自尊才能强迫他人尊敬你。

5. To know what people really think, pay regard to what they do rather than what they say.
   想知道别人真正的想法，注意他们做什么而不是说什么。

读书笔记

24 Stay Hungry, Stay Foolish B
求知若饥，虚心若愚 B

Steve Jobs
史蒂夫·乔布斯2005年在斯坦福大学毕业典礼上的著名演讲

It wasn't all **romantic**. I didn't have a dorm room, so I slept on the floor in friends' rooms. I returned coke bottles for the five cent **deposit**s to buy food with, and I would walk the seven miles across town every Sunday night to get one good meal a week at the Hare Krishna temple. I loved it. And much of what I **stumble**d into by following my curiosity and intuition turned out to be priceless later on. Let me give you one example:

Reed College at that time offered perhaps the best **calligraphy** instruction in the country. Throughout the campus every poster, every label on every drawer, was beautifully hand calligraphy. Because I had dropped out and didn't have to take the normal classes, I decided to take a calligraphy class to learn how to do this. I learned about serif and san serif typefaces, about **vary**ing the amount of space between different letter

这一点也不浪漫。我没有宿舍，所以我睡在友人家的地板上；那时可乐瓶的押金是五分钱，我把瓶子还回去好用押金买吃的。每个星期天晚上，我都步行七英里穿越市区，到Hare Krishna神庙吃一顿大餐。我喜欢那儿的食物。我跟随好奇心与直觉做的事，后来证明大多数都是极其珍贵的经验。举个例子吧：

当时里德学院提供全国最好的书法教育。校园里的每一张海报，每个抽屉的标签上，都是美丽的手写字。由于已经退学，我不用再去上那些常规课程，我想学如何写出一手漂亮字体。我学习了各种字体，学到在不同字母组合间变更字间距，以及如何做出漂亮的版式。那是一种科学永远无法捕捉的充满美感、历史感与艺术感的微妙，我觉得迷人极了。

combinations, about what makes great **typography** great. It was beautiful, historical, artistically **subtle** in a way that science can't capture, and I found it fascinating.

None of this had even a hope of any practical application in my life. But ten years later, when we were designing the first Macintosh computer, it all came back to me. And we designed it all into the Mac. It was the first computer with beautiful typography. If I had never dropped in on that single course in college, the "Mac" would have never had multiple typefaces or proportionally spaced fonts. And since Windows just copied the Mac, it's likely that no personal computer would have them. If I had never dropped out, I would have never dropped in on that calligraphy class, and personal computers might not have the wonderful typography that they do. Of course it was impossible to connect the dots looking forward when I was in college. But it was very, very clear looking backwards 10 years later.

Again, you can't connect the dots looking forward; you can only connect them looking backwards. So you have to trust that the dots will somehow connect in your future. You have to trust in something-your **gut**, destiny, life, **karma**, whatever-because believing that

我从没觉得学的这些东西能在我生活中起些什么实际作用，不过十年后，当我在设计第一款Macintosh电脑时，这些东西全都派上了用场，我把他们全都设计进了电脑里，这是第一台能排出好看版式的计算机。如果我当时没学这样一门课，Macintosh可能就不会有多重字体跟变间距字体了。自从Windows抄袭了Macintosh之后，所有的个人电脑都有了这些东西。如果我没有退学，就不会去书法班旁听，而今天的电脑大概就不会有出色的版式功能。当然，当我还在大学里时，不可能把这些点点滴滴预先联系在一起，但是这在十年后回顾，生命的轨迹就显得非常清楚。

再强调一次，你无法预见生命中点滴的串联；唯有未来回顾时，你才会明白那些点点滴滴是如何联系在一起的。所以你得相信，你现在所体会的东西，将来多少会联系在一起。你得信任某个东西，直觉也好，命运也好，生命也好，或者因果报应。这种做法让我不会失去希望，也让我的人生变得与众不同。

the dots will connect down the road will give you the confidence to follow your heart, even when it leads you off the well-worn path, and that will make all the difference.

单词解析 *Word Analysis*

romantic [rəʊˈmæntɪk] *adj.* 浪漫的；不切实际的 *n.* 浪漫的人
例 I was told that Spain is a romantic nation.
有人告诉我说，西班牙是个浪漫的国家。

deposit [dɪˈpɒzɪt] *v.* 放置；（使）沉淀；存储；付（订金等）；寄存 *n.* 存款；定金；堆积物；矿床
例 She deposited a pile of books on my desk.
她把一摞书放在我的书桌上。

stumble [ˈstʌmbl] *v.* 绊倒；蹒跚；犯错误；无意中发现 *n.* 绊倒；错误
例 I stumbled over a tree root.
我在一个树根上绊了一跤。

calligraphy [kəˈlɪɡrəfi] *n.* 书法
例 You can find books about calligraphy on that stack.
您可以在那个书架上找到有关书法的书。

vary [ˈveəri] *v.* 改变；变化；使多样化
例 Although this is the general approach, you can vary it to some degree.
尽管这是常规方法，但可以在一定程度上改变它。

typography [taɪˈpɒɡrəfi] *n.* （活版）印刷术；排印，印刷样式
例 Typography is the most important in this step.
印刷术在这一步最重要。

subtle [ˈsʌtl] *adj.* 微妙的；敏锐的；不明显的；精细的；狡猾的
例 There were subtle hints in his letter.

他的信中有些微妙的暗示。

gut [gʌt] *n.* 内脏；肠子；羊肠线；胆量；勇气
- He is a man with plenty of guts.
  他是个很有魄力的人。

karma ['kɑːmə] *n.*（佛教或印度教中）业；因果报应；缘分；命运
- I intend to release my karma to give power away.
  我意愿释放我送给别人力量的业力。

语法知识点 Grammar Points

① **And much of what I stumbled into by following my curiosity and intuition turned out to be priceless later on.**

这个句子中有一个结构"turn out to"，表示"结果是，原来是，证实是"。
- Master of Kungfu turned out to be a cheat.
  所谓的功夫大师结果是个骗子。

② **If I had never dropped in on that single course in college, the "Mac" would have never had multiple typefaces or proportionally spaced fonts.**

这个句子中有一个结构"would have done"，为用在虚拟语气中的过去将来完成时，表示与过去的事实相反。
- If I had seen him this afternoon, I would have told him about it.
  今天下午我要是见到他，我会告诉他那件事的。

③ **...because believing that the dots will connect down the road will give you the confidence to follow your heart, even when it leads you off the well-worn path, and that will make all the difference.**

这个句子中有一个结构"make the difference"，表示"有影响，很重要；产生差别"，等同于 be influential in。
- A few discussions, a few exchanges of ideas and a little tweaking here and there can make the difference between a

satisfied client and one who is not.
做一些讨论、构思和一些小调整会在满意的客户和不满意的客户之间产生差别。

经典名句 Famous Classics

1. No amount of anxiety makes any difference to anything that is going to happen.
   再多的焦虑也不能改变即将要发生的事。

2. Strength and growth come only through continuous effort and struggle.
   力量与成长只会来自持续的努力与奋斗。

3. I don't do anything unless I can give it 100%.
   除非我能 100% 投入，否则我不做任何事。

4. Gratitude can transform common days into thanksgivings, turn routine jobs into joy, and change ordinary opportunities into blessings.
   感恩可把普通的日子转化为感恩节，把例行工作转化为喜悦，把一般的机会化为祝福。

5. There's nothing enlightened about shrinking so that other people won't feel insecure around you. We are all meant to shine, as children do.
   缩小自己好让他人不会感到不安，一点都不明智，我们都应该像小孩般闪闪发亮。

读书笔记

25 Stay Hungry, Stay Foolish C
求知若饥，虚心若愚 C

Steve Jobs
史蒂夫·乔布斯2005年在斯坦福大学毕业典礼上的著名演讲

My second story is about love and loss.

I was lucky-I found what I loved to do early in life. Woz and I started Apple in my parents' **garage** when I was 20. We worked hard, and in 10 years Apple had grown from just the two of us in a garage into a two billion dollar company with over 4000 employees. We'd just **release**d our finest creation-the Macintosh-a year earlier, and I had just turned 30. And then I got fired.

How can you get fired from a company you started? Well, as Apple grew we hired someone who I thought was very talented to run the company with me, and for the first year or so things went well. But then our visions of the future began to **diverge** and eventually we had a falling out. When we did, our Board of Directors sided with him. And so at 30, I was out. And very publicly out. What had been the

我的第二个故事，有关爱与失去。

我非常幸运，年轻时就发现自己爱做什么事。我二十岁时，跟沃兹尼·艾克在我爸妈的车库里开创了苹果计算机的事业。我们拼命工作，苹果计算机在十年间从一间车库里的两个小伙子扩展成了一家员工超过四千人、市价二十亿美元的公司，在那之前一年推出了我们最棒的作品——Macintosh，而我才刚迈入人生的而立之年，就被炒了鱿鱼。

一个人怎么会被自己创办的公司炒鱿鱼呢？好吧，当苹果计算机成长后，我请了一个我以为他在经营公司上很有才干的家伙来，他在头几年也确实干得不错。可是我们对未来的愿景不同，最后只好分道扬镳，董事会站在他那边，炒了我鱿鱼，公开把我踢了出去。

focus of my entire adult life was gone, and it was **devastating**.

I really didn't know what to do for a few months. I felt that I had let the **previous** generation of **entrepreneur**s down-that I had dropped the **baton** as it was being passed to me. I met with David Packard and Bob Noyce and tried to apologize for screwing up so badly. I was a very public failure, and I even thought about running away from the valley. But something slowly began to dawn on me: I still loved what I did. The turn of events at Apple had not changed that one bit. I had been rejected, but I was still in love. And so I decided to start over.

I didn't see it then, but it turned out that getting fired from Apple was the best thing that could have ever happened to me. The heaviness of being successful was replaced by the lightness of being a beginner again, less sure about everything. It freed me to enter one of the most creative periods of my life. During the next five years, I started a company named NeXT, another company named Pixar, and fell in love with an amazing woman who would become my wife. Pixar went on to create the world's first computer-**animated** feature film, *Toy Story*, and is now the most successful animation studio in the world. In a remarkable turn of events, Apple bought

曾经是我整个成年生活重心的东西不见了,我不知所措,我失去了贯穿我成年生活的重心,遭受重创。

有几个月,我实在不知道要干什么好。我觉得我令企业界的前辈们失望了,我把他们交给我的接力棒弄丢了。我见了创办惠普的戴维·帕卡德和创办英特尔的鲍勃·诺伊斯,跟他们说我很抱歉把事情搞砸了。我成了人人皆知的失败者,我甚至想要离开硅谷。但是渐渐的,我发现,我还是喜爱我做的事情,在苹果经历的事件没有丝毫改变我爱做的事。我被否定了,但我的热忱不改,所以我决定从头来过。

当时我没发现,但是现在看来,被苹果开除,是我所经历过最好的事情。成功的沉重被凤凰涅槃的轻松所取代,每件事情都不那么确定,让我以自由之躯进入这辈子最有创意的阶段。接下来五年,我开了一家叫做NeXT的公司,又开一家叫做Pixar的公司,结识了后来成为我太太的曼妙女郎。Pixar接着制作了世界上第一部全计算机动画电影——《玩具总动员》——现在这家公司是世界上最成功的动画制作公司。然后,苹果买下了NeXT,

Stay Hungry, Stay Foolish C
求知若饥，虚心若愚 C

NeXT, and I returned to Apple, and the technology we developed at NeXT is at the heart of Apple's current **renaissance**. And Laurene and I have a wonderful family together.

我回到了苹果，我们在NeXT发展的技术成了苹果后来复兴的核心。我跟劳伦斯也拥有了幸福家庭。

单词解析 Word Analysis

garage ['gærɑːʒ] *n.* 汽车修理厂；车库 *v.* 把……放入车库

例 He sent his car to the garage for repair.
他把汽车送到修车厂修理。

release [rɪ'liːs] *n.* 释放；让渡；发行 *v.* 释放；让与；准予发表；发射

例 The prisoner was questioned before his release.
囚犯被释放之前受到了审问。

diverge [daɪ'vɜːdʒ] *v.* 分歧；分叉

例 Our views diverged so greatly that it was impossible to agree.
我们的观点存在着严重的分歧，绝无调和余地。

devastating ['devəsteɪtɪŋ] *adj.* 毁灭性的；破坏性的；惊人的；压倒性的；有魅力的

例 The area is subject to devastating seasonal winds.
这个地区常遭破坏性季风的袭击。

previous ['priːvɪəs] *adj.* 以前的；先于；在……之前

例 His previous attempts had been unsuccessful.
他以前的尝试没有成功。

entrepreneur [ˌɒntrəprə'nɜː(r)] *n.* 企业家；承包商；主办者

例 The entrepreneur has become a news figure.
这位企业家变成了新闻人物。

baton ['bætɒn] *n.* 指挥棒；接力棒；警棍；权杖；短棍

例 The conductor swept her baton through the air.

指挥家将她的指挥棒在空中挥舞。

animate ['ænɪmeɪt] *v.* 使有生气；赋予生命；鼓励 *adj.* 有生命的；有活力的

例 A smile animated her face.
一丝笑容使她脸上平添了生气。

renaissance [rɪ'neɪsns] *n.* 文艺复兴；再生

例 Her book captures the quintessence of Renaissance humanism.
她的书抓住了文艺复兴时期人文主义的精髓。

语法知识点 Grammar Points

① **Well, as Apple grew we hired someone who I thought was very talented to run the company with me...**

这个句子中有一个结构"run the company"，表示"经营公司"。

例 Career managers run the company for you - in theory.
职业经理替你经营这个公司——理论上是这样。

② **When we did, our Board of Directors sided with him.**

这个句子中有一个结构"side with"，表示"支持，站在……的一边"。

例 The public opinion believes that it shows China's firm support for the UN and multilateralism and indicates that China will always stand side by side with developing countries.
舆论普遍认为，这充分展示了中国对联合国和多边主义的坚定支持，表明中国始终与广大发展中国家站在一起。

③ **...I met with David Packard and Bob Noyce and tried to apologize for screwing up so badly.**

这个句子中有一个结构"screw up"，表示"拧紧；鼓舞；弄糟；狠狠地提高"。

例 This is an easy one to screw up.
这是一个很容易弄糟的错误。

Stay Hungry, Stay Foolish C
求知若饥，虚心若愚 C

经典名句 Famous Classics

1. If something is important enough, even if the odds are against you, you should still do it.
   如果一件事情够重要，即便成功的概率不高，你还是应该去做。

2. The measure of who we are is what we do with what we have.
   用自身的能力做了什么，是我们衡量自己的标准。

3. I don't count my sit-ups. I only start counting when it starts hurting. That is when I start counting, because then it really counts. That's what makes you a champion.
   我不数我做了几下仰卧起坐，只有痛的时候我才开始数。那时我才开始数，因为那才有意义，那才能让你成为冠军。

4. However difficult life may seem, there is always something you can do and succeed at.
   不管生活多么困难，总是有你可以做以及取得成功的事。

5. It's kind of fun to do the impossible.
   做不可能的事蛮有趣的。

读书笔记

26 Stay Hungry, Stay Foolish D
求知若饥，虚心若愚 D

Steve Jobs
史蒂夫·乔布斯2005年在斯坦福大学毕业典礼上的著名演讲

I'm pretty sure none of this would have happened if I hadn't been **fired** from Apple. It was awful tasting medicine, but I guess the patient needed it. Sometimes life's going to hit you in the head with a **brick**. Don't lose **faith**. I'm convinced that the only thing that kept me going was that I loved what I did. You've got to find what you love. And that is as true for your work as it is for your lovers.

Your work is going to fill a large part of your life, and the only way to be truly **satisfied** is to do what you believe is great work. And the only way to do great work is to love what you do. If you haven't found it yet, keep looking- and don't settle. As with all matters of the heart, you'll know when you find it. And like any great relationship, it just gets better and better as the years roll on. So keep looking-don't **settle**.

My third story is about death.

我很确定，如果当年苹果没开除我，这一切都不会在我身上发生。良药苦口，有时候，生活就像一块板砖拍向你的脑袋。不要丧失信心。我确信，我热爱我所做的事情，这就是这些年来让我继续走下去的唯一理由。你得找出你的最爱，对工作如此，对爱人亦是如此。

你的工作将占据你生命中相当大一部分，唯一获得真正满足的方法就是从事你认为具有非凡意义的工作，而从事一份伟大工作的唯一方法就是热爱你的工作。如果你还没找到这样一份工作，继续找，别停顿。全心全力，你知道你一定会找到。而且，如同任何伟大的浪漫关系一样，伟大的工作只会在岁月的酝酿中越陈越香。所以，在你找到之前，不要停下寻觅的脚步，不要停下。

Stay Hungry, Stay Foolish D
求知若饥，虚心若愚 D

When I was 17, I read a **quote** that went something like: "If you live each day as if it was your last, someday you'll most certainly be right." It made an impression on me, and since then, for the past 33 years, I've looked in the mirror every morning and asked myself: "If today were the last day of my life, would I want to do what I am about to do today?" And whenever the answer has been "No" for too many days in a row, I know I need to change something.

Remembering that I'll be dead soon is the most important tool I've ever **encounter**ed to help me make the big choices in life. Because almost everything-all **external** expectations, all pride, all fear of **embarrassment** or failure-these things just fall away in the face of death, leaving only what is truly important. Remembering that you are going to die is the best way I know to avoid the **trap** of thinking you have something to lose. You are already naked. There is no reason not to follow your heart.

我的第三个故事，是关于死亡。

当我十七岁时，我读到一则格言，好像是"把每一天都当成生命中的最后一天，你会发现每一天尽在掌握之中"。这对我影响深远，在过去33年里，我每天早上都会照镜子，自问："如果今天是此生最后一日，我今天要干些什么？"每当我连续太多天都得到"没事做"的答案时，我就知道我必须有所改变了。

提醒自己行将入土，是我在人生中下重大决定时所用过最重要的工具。因为几乎每件事——所有外界期望、所有名誉、所有对困窘或失败的恐惧——在面对死亡时，都消失了，只有最重要的东西才会留下。提醒自己快死了，是我所知的避免掉入畏惧失去这个陷阱里最好的方法。人生不带来，死不带去，没什么道理不顺心而为。

单词解析 *Word Analysis*

fire ['faɪə(r)] 开火；解雇；点燃；急速地连续说

例 He was fired by his boss.
他被他的老板解雇了。

brick [brɪk] *n.* 砖；砖块；砖状物 *v.* 用砖围砌（或堵）

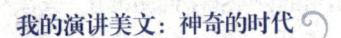

例 His new house was built by himself, brick by brick.
他的新房子是他自己一块砖一块砖砌起来的。

faith [feɪθ] *n.* 信仰；信念；信任

例 Christians profess their faith when they say the Creed.
基督教徒在念圣经时就表明了他们的宗教信仰。

satisfied ['sætɪsfaɪd] *adj.* 感到满意的

例 I'm not at all satisfied.
我一点也不满意。

settle ['setl] *v.* 解决；定居；安顿；平静；结算 *n.* 背长椅，座位；定居，安顿

例 If you pay for both of us now, we can settle up later.
你要是现在先付清咱们两人的账，事后咱俩再细算。

quote [kwəut] *v.* 引述；报价；举证 *n.* 引用

例 She asked the reporter not to quote her remarks.
她要求记者不要引述她的话。

encounter [ɪn'kaʊntə(r)] *n.* 意外的相见；邂逅；遭遇 *v.* 遭遇；遇到；偶然碰到

例 If both participate, it may be an actual encounter of bodiless consciousness.
如果是双向的，这会是一个真实的与灵魂的相见。

external [ɪk'stɜːnl] *adj.* 外来的；外部的；外面的；表面的 *n.* 外观；外部；外界事物

例 This news program only covers external events.
这一新闻节目只报道国外消息。

embarrassment [ɪm'bærəsmənt] *n.* 困窘；尴尬；难堪

例 Embarrassment caused the speaker to hesitate.
困窘使演讲人话语吞吐。

trap [træp] *n.* 圈套；陷阱；困境；*v.* 设圈套；陷入（困境）
- The police set a trap to catch the thief.
  警察设下了捉拿窃贼的圈套。

语法知识点 Grammar Points

① **And like any great relationship, it just gets better and better as the years roll on.**

这个句子中有一个结构"roll on"，表示"继续前进"，等同于keep moving。
- The Yellow River rolls on day and night.
  黄河日日夜夜地奔流不息。

② **...these things just fall away in the face of death, leaving only what is truly important.**

这个句子中有一个结构"in the face of"，表示"面对，在……面前"。
- The policemen bore up to their duty in the face of the terrorists.
  面对恐怖分子，警察始终忠于职守。

③ **There is no reason not to follow your heart.**

这个句子中有一个结构"There is no reason not to do sth."，表示"没有理由不做什么事"。
- At that time, there is no reason for me not to save you.
  那时，我没有理由不去救你。

经典名句 Famous Classics

1. To handle yourself, use your head; to handle others, use your heart.
   用大脑管理自己，用心对待别人。

2. Don't be so humble - you are not that great.
   别那么谦虚，你没那么伟大。

3. Plant your garden and decorate your own soul, instead of waiting

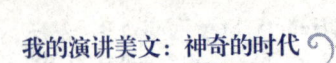

for someone to bring you flowers.
栽种你自己的花园并修饰自己的心灵，不要等人给你花朵。

4. Love is an act of will-namely, both an intention and an action. Will also implies choice. We do not have to love. We choose to love.
爱是意愿的实践——换句话说，它同时是一个意图和行为。意愿也意味着选择，我们不一定要爱，我们选择去爱。

5. Don't put limitations on yourself. Other people will do that for you.
别为自己设限，这点别人会帮你做。

读书笔记

27 Stay Hungry, Stay Foolish E
求知若饥，虚心若愚 E

Steve Jobs
史蒂夫·乔布斯2005年在斯坦福大学毕业典礼上的著名演讲

About a year ago I was **diagnosed** with cancer. I had a **scan** at 7:30 in the morning, and it clearly showed a **tumor** on my **pancreas**. I didn't even know what a pancreas was. The doctors told me this was almost certainly a type of cancer that is **incurable**, and that I should expect to live no longer than three to six months. My doctor advised me to go home and get my **affairs** in order, which is doctor's code for "prepare to die." It means to try and tell your kids everything you thought you'd have the next 10 years to tell them in just a few months. It means to make sure everything is buttoned up so that it will be as easy as possible for your family. It means to say your goodbyes.

I lived with that diagnosis all day. Later that evening I had a **biopsy**, where they stuck an **endoscope** down my throat, through my stomach into my **intestines**, put a needle into my pancreas

一年前，我被诊断出癌症。早上七点半我做了一个检查，扫描结果清楚地显示我的胰脏处出现一个肿瘤。我连胰脏是什么都不知道。医生告诉我，那几乎可以确定是一种不治之症，我大概活不到三到六个月了。医生建议我回家，把诸事安排妥当，这是医生对临终病人的标准建议。那代表你得试着在几个月内把你将来十年想跟子女讲的话讲完。那代表你得把每件事情搞定，尽可能减轻家人的负担。那意味着你告别时刻的来临。

我整天想着诊断结果，那天晚上做了一次切片，从喉咙伸入一个内视镜，从胃进肠子，将针探进胰脏，取了一些肿瘤细胞出来。我打了镇静剂，但是我的太太在场。她后来跟我说，当医生们用显微镜看过那些细胞后，他们都哭

and got a few cells from the tumor. I was **sedat**ed, but my wife, who was there, told me that when they viewed the cells under a microscope the doctors started crying because it turned out to be a very rare form of pancreatic cancer that is curable with surgery. I had the surgery and, thankfully, I'm fine now.

This was the closest I've been to facing death, and I hope it's the closest I get for a few more decades. Having lived through it, I can now say this to you with a bit more certainty than when death was a useful but purely intellectual concept: No one wants to die. Even people who want to go to heaven don't want to die to get there. And yet death is the destination we all share. No one has ever escaped it. And that is as it should be, because Death is very likely the single best invention of Life. It's Life's change agent. It clears out the old to make way for the new. Right now the new is you, but someday not too long from now, you will gradually become the old and be cleared away. Sorry to be so dramatic, but it's quite true.

了，因为那是非常少见的一种可以用手术治好的胰脏癌。所以我接受了手术，现在已经康复了。

这是我最接近死亡的时候，我希望那依然是未来几十年内最接近的一次。经历此事后，死亡对我来说只是一项有效的判断工具，并且只是一个纯粹的理性概念。我可以更肯定地告诉你们以下事实：没有人想死。即使那些想上天堂的人，也想活着上天堂。但是死亡是我们的人生终点站，没有人逃得过。这是注定的，因为死亡简直就是生命中最棒的发明，是生命更迭的媒介，送走老人们，给新生代留下空间。现在你们是新生代，但是不久的将来，你们也会逐渐变老，被送出人生的舞台。抱歉讲得这么戏剧化，但生命就是如此。

单词解析 Word Analysis

diagnose ['daɪəgnəuz] 判断；诊断（疾病）

例 What more will you want to know to diagnose this problem?
要弄清这个问题，你还需要知道些什么？

Stay Hungry, Stay Foolish E
求知若饥，虚心若愚 E

scan [skæn] *v.* 扫描；浏览；审视；细看 *n.* 扫描；浏览；细看

例 Could you teach me how to scan an image?
你可以教我如何扫描一个影像吗？

tumor ['tjuːmə] *n.* 肿瘤；肿块

例 The doctors decided to operate on him for the tumor.
医生们决定为他开刀切除肿瘤。

pancreas ['pæŋkriəs] *n.* 胰脏

例 Metastasis of renal cell carcinoma to the pancreas is uncommon.
肾细胞癌很少转移到胰脏。

incurable [ɪn'kjʊərəbl] *adj.* 不能医治的；不能矫正的；无救的 *n.* 不治的病人；无救的人

例 He was found in incurable disease.
他被查出得了不治之症。

affair [ə'feə(r)] *n.* 私通；事件；事务；事情

例 Their love affair is an open secret.
他们的风流韵事是公开的秘密。

biopsy ['baɪɒpsi] *n.* 活组织检查

例 The biopsy was taken from left forearm.
活组织检查的组织取自于左前臂。

endoscope ['endəskəʊp] *n.* 内窥镜；内诊镜

例 But the operation was not going smoothly. Schwarz's endoscope kept bumping into ice crystals that blurred the camera lens.
但是整个操作进行得并不顺畅，施瓦茨的内诊镜总是碰撞进冰晶里面弄糊摄影机镜片。

intestine [ɪn'testɪn] *n.* 肠

例 Vitamin K is not absorbed from the upper intestine.
维生素k不是从肠的上部吸收的。

sedate [sɪ'deɪt] *adj.* 安静的；镇静的 *v.* 使安静；使镇静

例 A sedate color scheme calls for an obvious place for the eye to rest.
一个安静的配色方案需要为眼睛提供一个显著的休息的地方。

语法知识点 Grammar Points

① About a year ago I was diagnosed with cancer.

这个句子中有一个结构 "be diagnosed with"，表示"被诊断为……病"。

例 Older patients are twice as likely to be diagnosed with thyroid cancer as younger patients.
老年患者被诊断为甲状腺癌的风险是年轻患者的两倍。

② My doctor advised me to go home and get my affairs in order...

这个句子中有一个结构 "get sth. in order"，表示"把……整理好，摆放整齐"。

例 They want to get affairs in order more for the benefit of those they love.
为了所爱的人，他们想让事情变得更井井有条。

The report is all buttoned up.
报告全部圆满完成了。

经典名句 Famous Classics

1. The problems that exist in the world today cannot be solved by the level of thinking that created them.
   今天世上的问题，无法由造成这些问题的思维所解决。

2. It's not the size of the dog in the fight; it's the size of the fight in the dog.
   狗打斗胜负取决不在于体型的大小，而是志气的大小。

3. The winner of the game is the player who makes the next-to-last mistake.

比赛的胜利者，是犯倒数第二个错误的人。

4. Encouragement is the oxygen of the soul.
   鼓励是灵魂的氧气。

5. Honor is self-esteem made visible in action.
   高尚就是行动中展现自尊。

读书笔记

28 Stay Hungry, Stay Foolish F
求知若饥，虚心若愚 F

Steve Jobs
史蒂夫·乔布斯2005年在斯坦福大学毕业典礼上的著名演讲

Your time is **limited**, so don't waste it living someone else's life. Don't be trapped by **dogma**-which is living with the results of other people's thinking. Don't let the noise of others' opinions **drown** out your own **inner** voice. And most important, have the courage to follow your heart and **intuition**. They somehow already know what you truly want to become. Everything else is secondary.

When I was young, there was an amazing **publication** called "The Whole Earth Catalog", which was one of the "bibles" of my generation. It was created by a fellow named Stewart Brand not far from here in Menlo Park, and he brought it to life with his poetic touch. This was in the late 60s, before personal computers and desktop publishing, so it was all made with typewriters, **scissor**s, and Polaroid cameras. It was sort of like Google in paperback form, 35

你们的时间有限，所以不要浪费时间活在别人的生活里。不要被教条所惑——盲从教条就是活在别人思考的结果里。不要让别人的意见淹没了你内在的心声。最重要的是，拥有跟随内心与直觉的勇气，它们可能已经知道你真正想要成为什么样的人。其他事物都是次要的。

在我年轻时，有本神奇的杂志叫做《全球概览》，风靡一时，被我们那一代人奉为神刊。创办人名叫斯图尔特·布兰德，他住在离这不远的门罗公园，他把这本杂志办得很有诗意。那是20世纪60年代末期，个人计算机和桌面发行系统还没出现，所有内容都是打字机、剪刀和拍立得相机做出来的。杂志内容有点像印在纸上的Google。但那是在Google出现的35年前：它富于理想

years before Google came along. It was idealistic, **overflow**ing with neat tools and great notions.

Stewart and his team put out several issues of *The Whole Earth Catalog*, and then when it had run its course, they put out a final issue. It was the mid-1970s, and I was your age. On the back cover of their final issue was a photograph of an early morning country road, the kind you might find yourself **hitchhik**ing on if you were so adventurous. Beneath it were the words: "Stay Hungry. Stay Foolish." It was their **farewell** message as they signed off. Stay Hungry. Stay Foolish. And I've always wished that for myself. And now, as you graduate to begin anew, I wish that for you.

Stay Hungry. Stay Foolish. Thank you all very much.

化,内容都是好用的工具与绝妙的见解。

斯图尔特跟他的出版团队出了好几期《全球概览》,快要无疾而终时,出了最后一期。当时是70年代中期,我正是在你们现在这个年龄的时候。在停刊号的封底,有张早晨乡间小路的照片,如果你喜欢搭车冒险,你会经常遇到这种乡间小路。在照片下有行小字:求知若饥,虚心若愚。那是他们亲笔写下的告别信息,我总是以此自许。现在在你们毕业,开始新生活之时,我也以此期许你们。

求知若饥,虚心若愚。非常感谢大家。

单词解析 *Word Analysis*

limited ['lɪmɪtɪd] *adj.* 有限的;被限制的

例 We had only limited communion with the natives.
我们与本地人的交往有限。

dogma ['dɒgmə] *n.* 教条;教义;信条

例 Beliefs have ossified into rigid dogma.
信仰已僵化为不可更动的教条。

drown [draʊn] *v.* 淹死;淹没

例 The little girl drowned in the river.

小女孩在河里淹死了。

inner [ˈɪnə(r)] *adj.* 内心的；内部的；里面的 *n.* 里面
例 He has no inner resources and hates being alone.
他没有内在的精神寄托，因而害怕孤独。

intuition [ˌɪntjuˈɪʃn] *n.* 直觉；直觉的知识
例 He takes his ground on intuition.
他的意见是凭直觉。

publication [ˌpʌblɪˈkeɪʃn] *n.* 出版；发行；出版物；公布；发表
例 The publication of his book will be next month.
将在下个月出版他的书。

scissor [ˈsɪzə] *n.* 剪刀
例 To practice scissor skills by cutting out large pictures and shapes.
能正确地使用剪刀，并能用剪刀剪大的形状和图片。

overflow [ˌəʊvəˈfləʊ] *v.* 泛滥；溢出；充满；洋溢 *n.* 泛滥；溢值；剩出
例 We must harness the rivers which overflow annually.
我们必须治理那些每年泛滥的河流。

hitchhiking [ˈhɪtʃhaɪkɪŋ] *n.* 搭乘；搭便车
例 I shouldn't have come with you on this silly hitchhiking trip.
我不应该和你一起做这个愚蠢的搭便车旅行。

farewell [ˌfeəˈwel] *n.* 告别 *adj.* 告别的
例 Farewell until we meet again!
下次再见！

语法知识点 Grammar Points

① **Don't be trapped by dogma.**

这个句子中有一个结构"be trapped by"，表示"被……困住"。
例 They were trapped by fire yesterday.
他们昨天被火困住。

② **Don't let the noise of others' opinions drown out your own inner voice.**

这个句子中有一个结构"drown out",表示"淹没"。

例 The actress's last few words were drowned out by applause.
女演员最后的几句话被掌声淹没了。

③ **...and he brought it to life with his poetic touch.**

这个句子中有一个结构"bring sth. to life",表示"使苏醒,使生动有趣"。

例 He brought his painting to life with his imagination.
他用想象使画作变得生动有趣。

④ **...they put out a final issue.**

这个句子中有一个结构"put out",表示"熄灭;伸出;出版;使不方便,打扰"。

例 The government has put out a statement denying these rumors.
政府发表了一项声明,否认了这些谣言。

经典名句 *Famous Classics*

1. Holiness, not happiness, is the chief end of man.
   圣洁,不是快乐,才是我们的最终目的。

2. Don't try to be perfect; just be an excellent example of a human being.
   别追求完美,成为人类的卓越典范即可。

3. Leadership is a two-way street, loyalty up and loyalty down. Respect for one's superiors; care for one's crew.
   领导有如双向道路,对上忠诚及对下忠诚,尊敬你的上司,照顾你的下属。

4. Neither a lofty degree of intelligence, nor imagination, nor both together, go to the making of genius. Love, love, love. That is the soul of genius.
   既不是代表智力的文凭、也不是想象力、也非两者加起来能促使天才产生,而是去爱、去爱、去爱,那是天才的灵魂。

5. We must accept finite disappointment, but we must never lose infinite hope.
   我们必须接受有限的失望,但绝不失去无尽的希望。

29 Never Selling Your Soul A
不要出卖自己的灵魂 A

Carly Fiorina
卡莉·菲奥莉娜

My fellow job seekers: I am honored to be among the first to congratulate you on completing your years at North Carolina A&T. But all of you should know: as Mother's Day gifts go, this one is going to be tough to beat in the years ahead.

But as you may have heard, I don't have that job anymore. After the news of my **departure** broke, I called the school and asked: do you still want me to come and be your **commencement** speaker?

Chancellor Renick put my fears to rest. He said, "Carly, if anything, you probably have more in common with these students now than you did before." And he's right. After all, I've been working on my **resume**. I've been lining up my references. I bought a new **interview** suit. If there are any recruiters here, I'll be free around November.

亲爱的毕业生们，我很荣幸成为首批恭贺你们顺利完成学业的人之一。大家必须明白：随着母亲节礼物的远离，在未来的岁月里，等待你们的将是艰难坎坷的日子。

你们也许已经听说了，我已经丢掉了现在的工作。在我离职的消息曝出以后，我给学校打电话问：你们还愿意让我来毕业典礼上发言吗？

Renick校长打消了我的顾虑。他说："卡莉，如果要说你现在与以前有什么不同的话，那就是你现在和这些毕业生们的共同性更多了。"确实如此。毕竟，我已经着手制作我的简历了。我已经开始投简历了。我还买了一件新的面试装。如果这儿有招聘人员的话，我大概11月的时候就自由了。

I want to thank you for having me anyway. This is the first public appearance I've made since I left HP. I wanted very much to be here because this school has always been set apart by something that I've believed very deeply; something that takes me back to the earliest memories I have in life.

One day at church, my mother gave me a small coaster with a saying on it. During my **entire** childhood, I kept this saying in front of me on a small desk in my room. In fact, I can still show you that coaster today. It says: "What you are is God's gift to you. What you make of yourself is your gift to God."

Those words have had a **huge impact** on me to this day. What this school and I believe in very deeply is that when we think about our lives, we shouldn't be limited by other people's **stereotypes** or **bigotry**. Instead, we should be motivated by our own sense of possibility. We should be motivated by our own sense of **accomplishment**. We should be motivated by what we believe we can become. Jesse Jackson has taught us; Ronald McNair taught us; the Greensboro Four taught us; that the people who focus on possibilities achieve much more in life than people who focus on limitations.

无论如何，我要感谢大家听我的演讲，这是我离开惠普之后的首次公开露面。我非常希望来到这里，因为这个学校由于我所坚信的一些东西而显得与众不同，这些东西把我带回到我生命中最初的记忆中去。

记得有一天，在教堂，母亲给了我一个小盘子，上面有一条谚语。在我整个童年时期，我将那条谚语摆放在房间的小书桌上，今天还可以把那个盘子拿给你们看。上面写着："你是什么由上帝决定，而你成为什么则是你献给上帝的礼物。"

这句话至今仍然对我有着巨大的影响。这个学校与我同样深信的是，当我们思考自己的生命时，不应该受到其他人的陈词滥调或偏见好恶的限制；相反，我们应该坚持自己对未来发展的判断，坚持自己对成就大业的把握，坚持对自己能有所作为的信念。Jesse Jackson的经历告诉我们，Ronald McNair的经历告诉我们，Greensboro Four的经历也告诉我们，注重发展性的人比注重局限性的人在生活中获得的要多得多。

Never Selling Your Soul A
不要出卖自己的灵魂 A

单词解析 Word Analysis

departure [dɪ'pɑːtʃə] *n.* 离开；背离，变更，违背；出发，起程；偏移，偏差
例 His departure was quite unexpected.
他这一走很出人意料。

commencement [kə'mensm(ə)nt] *n.* 开始，毕业典礼
例 The commencement was held in the grand hall.
毕业典礼在豪华的大厅举行。

resume [rɪ'zuːm] *n.* 摘要，梗概；简历 *v.* 重新开始，继续；重返；恢复
例 She resumed her maiden name after the divorce.
她离婚后重新使用娘家的姓。

interview ['ɪntə(r)vjuː] *n.* 面谈，接见，访问 *v.* 接见；会见
例 I've got an interview with National Chemicals.
我已获全国化学制品公司邀约面试。

entire [ɪn'taɪə] *adj.* 全体的，全部的，完全的
例 We are in entire agreement with you.
我们完全同意你的意见。

huge [hjuːdʒ] *adj.* 巨大的；无限的；极大的
例 Canada is a huge country.
加拿大是个幅员辽阔的国家。

impact ['ɪmpækt] *n.* 冲击，碰撞，撞击；影响 *v.* 挤入；压紧；撞击；冲击
例 He collapsed under the full impact of the blow.
他受到重击而倒下。

stereotype ['stɪrɪətaɪp] *n.* 铅版，老套，陈词滥调 *v.* 使用铅版，使一成不变
例 He doesn't conform to the usual stereotype of the city businessman with a dark suit and rolled umbrella.
他不像典型的城市商人那样，穿一身深色的套服、带一把收好的雨伞。

bigotry ['bɪɡətrɪ] *n.* 盲从；偏执，顽固
例 He deplored religious bigotry.

他谴责政治盲从。

accomplishment [əˈkʌmplɪʃm(ə)nt] *n.* 成就；教养；才艺；成绩；造诣

例 Dancing and singing were among her many accomplishments.
她多才多艺，能歌善舞。

语法知识点 Grammar Points

① **I am honored to be among the first to congratulate you on completing your years at North Carolina A&T.**

这个句子中有一个结构"I am honored to do/be..."，表示"我很荣幸能够……"。另外注意在某一地点，一般用介词at。

例 I am honored to deliver a speech here.
我很荣幸能够在此发表演讲。

② **Chancellor Renick put my fears to rest.**

这个句子中有一个结构"put sth. to rest"，表示"平息……，使……休息"。

例 Let's put him to rest.
我们需要让他休息。

③ **Carly, if anything, you probably have more in common with these students now than you did before.**

这个句子中有一个结构"have sth. in common with sb."，表示"与某人就某事有相似之处"，反义词组have nothing in common with sb.。

例 I have something in common with him.
我和他有诸多相似之处。

④ **I wanted very much to be here because this school has always been set apart by something that I've believed very deeply; something that takes me back to the earliest memories I have in life.**

这个句子中有两个结构"be set apart."和"take sb. to sp."，分别表示"使分离，区别"和"带某人去某地"。这里be set apart的意思是与众不同。

例 His accent sets him apart.
他的口音让他与众不同。

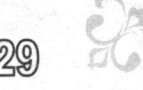

I want to take my mom to America.
我想带我妈妈去美国。

⑤ **Those words have had a huge impact on me to this day.**

这个句子中有一个结构"have an impact on sth.",表示"对……有影响"。同义词组还有have an influence on sth.。

例 God has a huge impact on my life.
上帝对我的生活影响很大。

经典名句 Famous Classics

1. Do not keep anything for a special occasion, because every day that you live is a special occasion.
别为某个所谓的特别时刻而有所保留,因为你生活的每一天都是那么特别。

2. Both happiness and sadness in our life would fade away with time.
生命中无论快乐还是悲伤,终将随时光一起逝去。

3. The best things in life are free. The second best are very expensive.
生命中最美好的事物都是免费的,第二美好的事物都很贵。

4. What makes life dreary is the want of a motive.
没有了目的,人生便暗淡无光。

5. The soul is not where it lives, but it loves.
爱之所在,亦心之所在。

30 Never Selling Your Soul B
不要出卖自己的灵魂 B

Carly Fiorina
卡莉·菲奥莉娜

The question for all of you today is: how will you **define** what you make of yourself? To me, what you make of yourself is actually two questions. There's the "you" that people see on the outside. And that's how most people will **judge** you, because it's all they can see. But then, there's the **invisible** you, the "you" on the inside. For 25 years, when people have asked me for career advice, what I always tell them is don't give up what you have inside. Never sell your soul, because no one can ever pay you back.

What I mean by not selling your soul is don't be someone you're not, don't be less than you are, don't give up what you believe, because whatever the **consequences** that may seem **scary** or bad-whatever the consequences of staying true to yourself are-they are much better than the consequences of selling your soul.

You have been tested **mightily** in

今天大家都面临着一个问题：如何定义自己是什么样的人？在我看来，你想成为什么样的人实际上涉及两个问题。一个是人们从表面上看到的"你"。多数人会以此来评判你，因为那是他们所能看到的全部。不过还有一个看不见的你，一个内在的"你"。25年来，人们向我求教职业建议时，我总是告诉他们不要放弃你的内在本性，不要出卖你的灵魂，因为没有人能够支付得起。

我所说的不要出卖灵魂是指，不要违背自己的本性，不要掩盖自己的天赋，也不要放弃自己的信念，因为不论后果看上去如何可怕或糟糕，无论保持自己的本色会产生怎样的后果——这总比出卖灵魂好得多。

大家到达人生这一刻之前已经饱经考验。你们心里都比我清楚，从离开校园的这

your life to get to this moment. And all of you know much better than I do: from the moment you leave this campus, you will be tested. You will be tested because you won't fit some people's pre-**conceived notions** or stereotypes of what you're supposed to be, of who you're supposed to be. People will have stereotypes of what you can or can't do, of what you will or won't do, of what you should or shouldn't do. But they only have power over you if you let them have power over you. They can only have **control** if you let them have control, if you give up what's inside.

一刻起，你们还要面临考验。有的考验是由于你们不符合一些人预想的观念，不符合他们对你们本该做什么工作、成为什么样的人的模式化的看法。人们对你们的能力高低、意愿以及什么该做什么不该做都有模式化的看法。不过除非你们屈服，否则他们对你们没有任何影响力。除非你们让他们控制，放弃你们的内在本性，否则他们无法控制你们。

单词解析 Word Analysis

define [dɪˈfaɪn] *v* 定义；详细说明

例 It's hard to define exactly what has changed.
很难解释清楚到底发生了什么变化。

judge [dʒʌdʒ] *n* 法官，推事，审判官 *v* 审理；判断；鉴定；下判断；作评价

例 Judging from previous experience, he will be late.
根据以往的经验来看，他得迟到。

invisible [ɪnˈvɪzəbl] *adj* 看不见的；无形的

例 There is visible labor and invisible labor.
有有形的劳动和无形的劳动。

consequence [ˈkɒnsɪkwəns] *n* 结果；推论；推理

例 Her investment had disastrous consequences: she lost everything she owned.
她的投资结果很惨，血本无归。

我的演讲美文：神奇的时代

scary ['skerɪ] *adj.* 容易受惊的，提心吊胆的，胆小的

例 I like to dress up as nice clowns and scary ones.
我喜欢装扮成善解人意但很胆小的小丑。

mightily ['maɪtɪlɪ] *adv.* 强有力地，激烈地，勇猛地；非常，极其

例 We labored mightily to rebuild the walls.
我们非常卖力地工作建墙。

conceive [kən'siːv] *v.* 构思；持有；以为；构想，设想；怀孕

例 It was then that I conceived the notion of running away.
就在那时我产生了逃跑的念头。

notion ['nəʊʃn] *n.* 概念，想法，观念

例 Your head is full of silly notions.
你满脑子都是糊涂思想。

control [kən'trəʊl] *n.* 控制，克制，管理 *v.* 控制；管理；支配；克制

例 He has no control over his emotions.
他控制不住自己的感情。

语法知识点 Grammar Points

① ...whatever the consequences that may seem scary or bad-whatever the consequences of staying true to yourself are-they are much better than the consequences of selling your soul.

这个句子中有一个结构 "stay true to sb."，表示"忠实于某人，对某人真诚"。stay可以换成be。

例 If you want to make friends, you have to stay true to others.
如果你想交朋友，你要待人真诚。

② You will be tested because you won't fit some people's pre-conceived notions or stereotypes of what you're supposed to be, of who you're supposed to be.

这个句子中有一个结构 "be supposed to be/do"，表示"应该"，相当于should。

Never Selling Your Soul B
不要出卖自己的灵魂 B

例 You are supposed to leave at the moment.
你此时该走了。

③ They can only have control if you let them have control, if you give up what's inside.

这个句子中有两个结构"let sb.do sth."和"give up",分别表示"让某人做某事"和"放弃"。前者使役动词还有make,后者give up可以和介词on搭配。

例 I would not have let you go.
我本不想让你走的。

I don't want to give up.
我不想放弃。

经典名句 Famous Classics

1. Life is like an onion; you peel it off one layer at a time, and sometimes you weep.
   生活就像个洋葱,你只能一层一层剥开它,还不时地流泪。

2. Winter is an etching, spring a watercolor, summer an oil painting and autumn a mosaic of them all.
   冬天是蚀刻画,春天是水彩画,夏天是油画,而秋天则是三者的美丽交织。

3. Never regret anything because at one time it was exactly what you wanted.
   不要后悔做任何事情,因为曾经有个时候,那正是你想要的。

4. Trust no one because even your shadow will leave you in darkness.
   不要过分信赖别人,即便是你的影子,也会在黑暗中离开你。

5. Whether it is happiness or sorrow, it would finally become memories of life.
   一生中无论快乐与悲伤,最后都将成为回忆。

31 Never Selling Your Soul C
不要出卖自己的灵魂 C

Carly Fiorina
卡莉·菲奥莉娜

At every step along the way, your soul will be tested. Every test you pass will make you stronger. But let's not be **naive**. Sometimes, there are consequences to "not selling your soul". Sometimes, there are consequences to "staying true to what you believe". And sometimes, those consequences are very difficult. But as long as you understand the consequences and **accept** the consequences, you are not only stronger. As a result, you're more at peace.

Many people have asked me how I feel now that I've lost my job. The truth is, I'm proud of the life I've lived so far, and **though** I've made my share of mistakes, I have no regrets. The worst thing I could have imagined happened. I lost my job in the most public way, and the press had a field day with it all over the world. And guess what? I'm still here. I am at peace and my soul is **intact**. I could have given it away and the story

在人生的每一步，灵魂都会受到考验。每通过一次考验你都会变得更加坚强。但是我们也不能幼稚。有时不出卖灵魂会影响你们。有时坚持自己的信念也会影响你们。有时这些影响使你们非常为难。然而只要你们理解并接受这些影响，你们不仅会更加坚强，而且会更加心安……

很多人问我如今失去了工作有何感受。说实话，到目前为止我对自己的生活经历引以为豪，虽然也犯过错误，但是我毫不遗憾。我能想象到的最糟糕的事发生了。我在众目睽睽之下丢了工作，全世界媒体大肆报道。大家猜怎么着了？我依旧在这里。我心安理得，灵魂完整无缺。我本可以出卖灵魂，那么我的故事就会改写。可是我的脑海里响起了《圣经》里的话："如果你得

would be different. But I heard the word of **Scripture** in my head: "What benefit will it be to you if you gain the whole world, but lose your soul?"

When people have stereotypes of what you can't do, show them what you can do. When they have stereotypes of what you won't do, show them what you will do. Every time you pass these tests, you learn more about yourself. Every time you **resist** someone else's smaller notion of who you really are, you test your courage and your endurance. Each time you **endure** and stay true to yourself, you become stronger and better.

Never sell your education short. And the fact that this school believed in you means you should never sell yourself short. What I have learned in 25 years of managing people is that everyone **possesses** more potential than they realize. Living life defined by your own sense of possibility, not by others' notions of limitations, is the path to success.

到整个世界却失去自己的灵魂，那又有什么好处？"

当人们对你抱有成见，认为你无法做某事时，你就让他们看看你能做什么。当他们认为你不愿做某事时，你就要向他们展现自己愿意做的事。每次你通过这种考验，你对自己的认识就加深了一层。每当你抵制别人贬低真实的你的时候，你就在考验自己的胆量和耐力。每当你坚持下来，保持自我，你就更加坚强和优秀。

不要低估你所受教育的价值。这所学校对你们有信心，你们就不能低估自身的价值。我从事人力管理工作25年，我的心得是每个人都具有自身不曾意识到的潜能。按自己对未来发展的设想去生活，不要被别人的观念束缚住手脚，这才是成功之道。

单词解析 Word Analysis

naive [naɪ'iːv] *adj.* 天真的，幼稚的

例 You weren't so naive as to believe him, were you?
你没有轻易相信他，是吧？

accept [ək'sept] *v.* 领受，接受；认可；同意

例 The college I applied to has accepted me.
我报了名的学院已经录取我了。

though [ðəʊ] *conj.* 虽然；尽管 *adv.* 虽然，可是

例 She won first prize, though none of us had expected it.
她得了头奖，虽然这件事我们都没想到。

intact [ɪn'tækt] *adj.* 尚未被人碰过的，完整的

例 He can scarcely survive this scandal with his reputation intact.
他经此丑闻名誉很难不受损。

Scripture ['skrɪptʃə(r)] *n.* 圣经；圣经中的片段

例 I love reading Scripture.
我喜欢读《圣经》。

resist [rɪ'zɪst] *n.* 防染剂；抗蚀剂 *v.* 抵抗，抗，反抗；抵抗

例 He was charged with resisting arrest.
他被控拒捕。

endure [ɪn'djʊə] *v.* 忍耐，忍受；容忍

例 I can't endure to see/seeing children suffer.
看着儿童受苦，我可受不了。

possess [pə'zes] *v.* 拥有，持有；占有

例 They possess property all over the world.
他们在世界各地均拥有财产。

语法知识点 *Grammar Points*

① **But as long as you understand the consequences and accept the consequences, you are not only stronger. As a result, you're more at peace.**

这两个句子中有三个结构"as long as"，"as a result"和"at peace"，分别表示"只要""结果"和"和平"的意思。As long as的同义词组是so long as；as a result相当于as a consequence；at peace可以用peaceful来替换。

例 As long as you love me, I will stay with you and as a result we will form a family together and stay at peace.
只要你爱我，我就会一直和你在一起。然后，我们组建家庭，和平无忧。

② **The truth is, I'm proud of the life I've lived so far, and though I've made my share of mistakes, I have no regrets.**

这个句子中有两个结构"be proud of"和"so far"，分别表示"对……很自豪"以及"到目前为止"。

例 She is proud of herself.
她为自己感到骄傲。

So far, there is only one credible proposal.
到目前为止，只有一个可靠的建议。

③ **I could have given it away and the story would be different.**

这个句子中有一个结构"give it away"，表示"放弃"。这句话里存在虚拟语气，could have done表示本可以做……却没有做……。

例 I will never give it away and I will hang on there.
我永不放弃并坚持不懈。

④ **Every time you pass these tests, you learn more about yourself.**

这个句子中有一个结构"learn more about..."，表示"了解更多……"。这句话里Every time引导了一个时间状语从句，表示每次你做某事，会如何如何。

例 I want to learn more about this boy.
我想多了解一下这个男孩。

⑤ **Living life defined by your own sense of possibility, not by others' notions of limitations, is the path to success.**

这个句子中有一个结构"the path to..."，表示"去……的道路"。这句话里动名词ing做主语。

例 She didn't know the path to your home.
她不知道去你家的路。

经典名句 Famous Classics

1. Be it ever so humble, there is no place like home.
休嫌它寒微贫贱，天涯无处似家园。

2. They always say time changes everything, but you actually have

to change it yourself.
人们总说时间会改变一切，但事实上，你必须自己去改变一切。

3. Sometimes you need to look at life from a different perspective.
有时候，你需要换个角度看生活。

4. Cherish every moment with those you love at every stage of your journey.
人生的每个阶段，都要珍惜和所爱的人在一起的每一刻。

5. Everyone is a moon, and has a dark side which he never shows to anybody.
每个人都像月亮，都有着不愿示人的一面。

读书笔记

32 Never Selling Your Soul D
不要出卖自己的灵魂 D

Carly Fiorina
卡莉·菲奥莉娜

Starting today, you are one of the most **promising** things America has to offer: you are an Aggie with a degree.

My hope is that you live life defined by your own sense of possibility, your own sense of **worth**, your own sense of your soul. Define yourself for yourself, not by how others are going to define you, and then stick to it. Find your own internal **compass**. I use the term compass, because what does a compass do? When the winds are howling, and the storm **raging**, and the sky is so cloudy you have nothing to navigate by, a compass tells you where true North is. And I think when you are in a lonely situation; you have to **rely** on that compass. Who am I? What do I believe? Do I believe I am doing the right thing for the right **reason** in the best way that I can? Sometimes, that's all you have. And always, it will be enough.

Most people will judge you by what

从今天开始，你们就是美国培养出的最有前途的人：获得学位的农学院毕业生。

我希望大家能够按照自己对未来的设想、对价值的把握、对自己灵魂的坚持来生活。为自己制定目标，不要因别人如何界定你就做出改变，要坚持这个目标不放松。找到自己内心的指南针。我用指南针这个词，指南针是做什么的？狂风大作、暴雨倾盆、阴云密布之时，你没有任何可以用来导航的东西，指南针就能告诉你真正的北方在哪里。我想当你孤独无助之时，你必须要依靠这个指南针。我是谁？我相信什么？我认为自己正在为正确的目标，以尽可能好的方式做正确的事吗？有时这就是你所拥有的全部。而且它本身往往就够用了。

大多数人凭外在的表现

they see on the outside. Only you and God will know what's on the inside. But at the end of your life, if people ask you what your greatest accomplishment was, my guess is, it will be something that happened inside you, that no one else ever saw, something that had nothing to do with outside **success**, and everything to do with how you **decide** to live in the world.

What you are today is God's gift to you. What you make of yourself is your gift to God. He is waiting for that gift right now. Make it something **extraordinary**.

来评判你。只有你和上帝才知道你的内在本性。然而在生命最后一刻，假如人们问起你最大的成就，我猜那将是发生在你内心的某些体验，谁都不曾见过，与外在的成功也毫无关系，那不过是你对如何在这个世界生活所做出的决定。

你们现在的样子是上帝的馈赠，你将来什么样子是对上帝的回报。此刻上帝正在等待你的回报。让你的回报非同凡响吧！

单词解析 Word Analysis

promising ['prɑmɪsɪŋ] *adj.* 有希望的，前途有望的
例 He is a promising young actor.
他是一个前途无量的演员。

worth [wɜːθ] *n.* 价值，财产 *adj.* 值钱的，值的看中的
例 Our house is worth about 60000.
我们的房子约值60000英镑。

compass ['kʌmpəs] *n.* 罗盘；圆规；指南针；境界；周围 *v.* 图谋，计划；达到，获得；包围；理解
例 Use your compass to bisect an angle.
用圆规把一个角二等分。

rage [reɪdʒ] *n.* 狂怒，盛怒；强烈的欲望 *v.* 发怒，怒斥；流行，盛行
例 Her rages don't last long.
她发脾气很快就消气。

rely [rɪ'laɪ] *v.* 依靠，依赖；信赖，相信；依仗；指望

例 She cannot be relied on to tell the truth.
别指望她能说真话。

success [sək'ses] *n.* 成功；胜利；成就；成功的事

例 Her rapid rise to the top has been one of the film industry's most remarkable success stories.
她迅速走红是电影界最杰出的一个事例。

decide [dɪ'saɪd] *v.* 决定；使下决心；决意；使决断；决定

例 It's difficult to decide between the two.
很难在这两者之间决定取舍。

extraordinary [ɪk'strɔːdnrɪ] *adj.* 非常的；非凡的；特别的

例 Her talents are quite extraordinary.
她才华出众。

语法知识点 Grammar Points

① **Starting today, you are one of the most promising things America has to offer: you are an Aggie with a degree.**

这个句子中有一个结构"one of..."，表示"……的其中一个"，one of后面加可数名词复数形式。

例 I am one of the top students in my class.
我是班里的其中一个优等生。

② **Define yourself for yourself, not by how others are going to define you, and then stick to it.**

这个句子中有两个结构"be going to"和"stick to"，分别表示"将要，打算"和"坚持，谨守"。前者同义词还有will，用于将来时态，但是没有打算、计划的意味；后者坚持stick to的同义词组还有follow、stay close to和stick with。

例 I am going to visit the Great Wall tomorrow.
我明天要去参观长城。

You have to stick to your dream!
坚持自己的梦想别动摇！

> ③ And I think when you are in a lonely situation; you have to rely on that compass.

这个句子中有一个结构 "rely on..."，表示"依赖，依靠，取决于"，相当于 depend on 和 rely upon。

例 I relied on you(r) coming early.
我指望你早来。

> ④ ...something that had nothing to do with outside success, and everything to do with how you decide to live in the world.

这个句子中有一个结构 "had nothing/something to do with..."，表示"和……无关/有关"。

例 I hope she has nothing to do with this.
我希望她与此事无关。

经典名句 Famous Classics

1. Life is tough, and if you have the ability to laugh at it you have the ability to enjoy it.
   人生很艰难，如果你有笑对人生的能力，你就有享受人生的能力。

2. Do not worry about winning or losing; think of what you will gain.
   别为输赢而纠结，想想你能收获什么吧。

3. Why waste precious time dreaming when waking life is so much better?
   醒着的生活如此美好，为何要把时间浪费在做梦上呢?

4. The best makeup is Smile. The best jewelry is Modesty. The best clothing is Confidence.
   最好的妆容是微笑，最好的饰品是谦虚，最好的衣裳是自信。

5. Never give up on something you really want. It's difficult to wait, but worse to regret.
   永远不要放弃你真正想要的东西。等待虽难，但后悔更甚。

33 Amazing Time A
神奇的时代 A

Bill Gates
比尔·盖茨

The defining and ongoing innovations of this age-biotechnology, the computer, the Internet: give us a chance we've never had before to end **extreme** poverty and end death from preventable disease.

The emergence of low-cost personal computers gave rise to a powerful network that has **transformed** opportunities for learning and communicating.

The magical thing about this network is not just that it **collapses** distance and makes everyone your neighbor. It also dramatically **increases** the number of brilliant minds we can have working together on the same problem-and that scales up the rate of innovation to a staggering degree.

At the same time, for every person in the world who has access to this technology, five people don't. That means many creative minds are left out of this

这个时代无时无刻不在涌现出革新——生物技术、计算机、互联网——它们给了我们一个从未有过的机会，去终结那些极端的贫穷和非恶性疾病的死亡。

低成本个人电脑的出现，使得一个强大的互联网有机会诞生，它为学习和交流提供了巨大的机会。

网络的神奇之处，不仅仅是它缩短了物理距离，使得天涯若比邻。它还极大地增加了使怀有共同想法的人们聚集在一起的机会，我们可以为了解决同一个问题，一起工作。这就大大加快了革新的进程，发展速度简直快得让人震惊。

与此同时，世界上有条件上网的人，只是全部人口的六分之一。这意味着，还有许多具有创造性的人们没有加入

discussion: smart people with practical intelligence and **relevant** experience who don't have the technology to hone their talents or contribute their ideas to the world.

We need as many people as possible to have **access** to this technology, because these advances are triggering a revolution in what human beings can do for one another. They are making it possible not just for national governments, but for universities, corporations, smaller organizations, and even individuals to see problems, see approaches and measure the **impact** of their efforts to address the hunger, poverty and desperation George Marshall spoke of 60 years ago.

Members of the Harvard Family: Here in the Yard is one of the great collections of intellectual talent in the world.

What for?

There is no question that the faculty, the alumni, the students and the benefactors of Harvard have used their power to improve the lives of people here and around the world. But can we do more? Can Harvard **dedicate** its intellect to improving the lives of people who will never even hear its name?

Let me make a request of the deans and the professors-the intellectual leaders here at Harvard: As you hire

到我们的讨论中来。那些有着实际的操作经验和相关经历的聪明人，却没有技术来帮助他们，将他们的天赋或者想法与全世界分享。

我们要尽可能地让更多的人有机会使用新技术，因为这些新技术正在引发一场革命，人类将因此可以互相帮助。新技术正在创造一种可能，让不仅是政府，还包括大学、公司、小机构甚至个人，能够发现问题所在、找到解决办法、评估他们努力的效果，去改变那些马歇尔六十年前就说到过的问题——饥饿、贫穷和绝望。

哈佛是一个大家庭。这个院子里在场的人们，是全世界最有智慧的群体之一。

我们可以做些什么？

毫无疑问，哈佛的老师、校友、学生和资助者，已经用他们的能力改善了世界各地人们的生活。但是，我们还能够再做什么呢？有没有可能，哈佛的人们可以将他们的智慧，用来帮助那些甚至从来没有听到过"哈佛"这个名字的人？

请允许我向各位院长和教授提出一个请求——你们是哈佛的智力领袖，当你们雇用新的老师、授予终身教职、评估

new faculty, award tenure, review curriculum and determine degree **requirements**, please ask yourselves: Should our best minds be dedicated to solving our biggest problems?

课程、决定学位颁发标准的时候，请问自己如下的问题：我们最优秀的人才是否在致力于解决我们最大的问题？

单词解析 Word Analysis

extreme [ɪk'striːm] *n.* 极端，末端 *adj.* 极端的，偏激的，尽头的

例 His ideas are too extreme for me.
我认为他的思想太偏激了。

transform [træns'fɔrm] *v.* 转换，改造，改变；变换，转化

例 A fresh coat of paint can transform a room.
房间重新粉刷一遍可大为改观。

collapse [kə'læps] *n.* 倒塌；失败；崩溃 *v.* 倒塌；瓦解；崩溃；使倒塌

例 The enterprise collapsed through lack of support.
该企业因缺少支持而倒闭。

increase [ɪn'kriːs] *n.* 增加，利益，增进 *v.* 增加；繁殖；加大

例 He increased his speed to overtake the lorry.
他加大速度以超过前面的货车。

relevant ['relɪvənt] *adj.* 有关的；恰当的；切题的；有意义的

例 Colour and sex are hardly relevant when appointing somebody to a job.
肤色和性别对于任命某人担任某职来说没有什么关系。

access ['ækses] *n.* 接近；使用；接近的机会 *v.* 取出；接近；使用

例 Students must have access to a good library.
学生要有使用好图书馆的便利条件。

impact ['ɪmpækt] *n.* 冲击，碰撞，撞击；影响 *v.* 挤入；压紧；撞击；冲击

例 Her speech made a tremendous impact on everyone.
她的演说对大家震动很大。

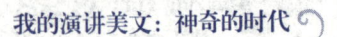

dedicate ['dedɪkeɪt] *v.* 献；题献；致力

例 She dedicated her first book to her husband.
她把自己的第一本书献给了丈夫。

requirement [rɪ'kwaɪə(r)mənt] *n.* 需求，要求，必要条件

例 The new computer system will meet all our requirements.
新电脑系统会满足我们所有的要求。

语法知识点 *Grammar Points*

① **The emergence of low-cost personal computers gave rise to a powerful network that has transformed opportunities for learning and communicating.**

这个句子中有一个结构"give rise to sth."，表示"引起；使发生"，同义词组还有result in和lead to。

例 Her disappearance gave rise to the wildest rumors.
她失踪一事引起了各种流言蜚语。

② **It also dramatically increases the number of brilliant minds we can have working together on the same problem-and that scales up the rate of innovation to a staggering degree.**

这个句子中有两个结构"work on sth."和"scale up"，分别表示"继续工作；影响；设法说服"和"扩大规模"，后者反义词是scale down。

例 We can work on this together.
我们可以一起解决这个问题。
We've scaled up production to meet demand.
我们已经扩大了生产以满足需求。

③ **At the same time, for every person in the world who has access to this technology, five people don't.**

这个句子中有一个结构"have access to sth."，表示"（使用某物或接近某人）机会或权利"，同义词组还有get access to do sth.。

例 Only high officials had access to the president.
只有高级官员才可以接近总统。

④ **Can Harvard dedicate its intellect to improving the lives of people who will never even hear its name?**

这个句子中有一个结构"dedicate...to...",表示"将(自己、时间、精力等)奉献给(崇高的事业或目的)",同义词组还有devote...to...,比如devote oneself to a noble cause表示献身于一项崇高的事业。这里的to是介词,后面要用名词或者动名词。

例 She dedicated her life to helping the poor.
她毕生致力于帮助穷人。

经典名句 *Famous Classics*

1. The supreme happiness of life is the conviction that we are loved. —Victor Hugo
生活中最大的幸福是坚信有人爱我们。(维克多·雨果)

2. Spread love everywhere you go. Let no one ever come to you without leaving happier.
无论你去哪里,都要让每一个来找你的人离开时都比之前更快乐些。

3. Men are nearly always willing to believe what they wish. —Julius Caesar
人总爱想入非非,把愿望变成现实。(恺撒大帝)

4. Don't argue with the people of strong determination, because they may change the fact. —Shakespeare
别和意志坚定的人争辩,因为他们可以改变事实!(莎士比亚)

5. Man cannot discover new oceans unless he has courage to lose sight of the shore. —Gide
人只有鼓起勇气告别海岸,才能发现新的海洋。(纪德)

34 Amazing Time B
神奇的时代 B

Bill Gates
比尔·盖茨

Should Harvard encourage its faculty to take on the world's worst inequities? Should Harvard students learn about the depth of global poverty...the **prevalence** of world hunger...the **scarcity** of clean water...the girls kept out of school...the children who die from diseases we can cure?

Should the world's most **privileged** people learn about the lives of the world's least privileged?

These are not **rhetorical** questions-you will answer with your policies.

When you consider what those of us here in this Yard have been given-in talent, privilege, and opportunity-there is almost no limit to what the world has a right to expect from us.

In line with the promise of this age, I want to **exhort** each of the graduates here to take on an issue-a complex problem, a deep inequity and become

哈佛是否鼓励她的老师去研究解决世界上最严重的不平等？哈佛的学生是否了解全球那些极端的贫穷……世界性的饥荒……清洁的水资源的缺乏……无法上学的女童……死于非恶性疾病的儿童？

那些世界上过着最优越生活的人们，了解那些最困难的人们的生活吗？

这些问题并非修辞语言，你必须用自己的行动来回答。

想一想吧，我们在这个院子里的这些人，被给予过什么——天赋、特权、机遇——那么可以这样说，全世界的人们几乎有无限的权利，期待我们做出贡献。

同这个时代的期望一样，我也要向今天各位毕业的同学提出一个忠告：你们要选择一个问题，一个复杂的问题，一个

a specialist on it. If you make it the focus of your career, that would be **phenomenal**. But you don't have to do that to make an impact. For a few hours every week, you can use the growing power of the Internet to get informed, find others with the same interests, see the **barriers** and find ways to cut through them.

You graduates are coming of age in an amazing time. As you leave Harvard, you have technology that members of my class never had. You have **awareness** of global inequity, which we did not have. And with that awareness, you likely also have an informed conscience that will **torment** you if you abandon these people whose lives you could change with very little effort. You have more than we had; you must start sooner and carry on longer.

Knowing what you know, how could you not?

And I hope you will come back here to Harvard 30 years from now and reflect on what you have done with your talent and your energy. I hope you will judge yourselves not on your professional accomplishments alone, but also on how well you have addressed the world's deepest inequities...on how well you treated people a world away

有关于人类深刻的不平等的问题，然后你们要变成这个问题的专家。如果你们能够使得这个问题成为你们职业的核心，那么你们就会非常杰出。但是，你们不一定要去做那些大事。每个星期只用几个小时，你就可以通过互联网得到信息，找到志同道合的朋友，发现困难所在，找到解决它们的途径。

在座的各位毕业的同学，你们所处的时代是一个神奇的时代。当你们离开哈佛的时候，你们拥有的技术，是我们那一届学生所没有的。你们已经了解到了世界上的不平等，我们那时还不知道这些。有了这样的了解之后，要是你再弃那些你可以帮助的人们于不顾，就将受到良心的谴责。只需一点小小的努力，你就可以改变那些人的生活。你们比我们拥有更大的能力，你们必须尽早开始，尽可能长时期坚持下去。

知道了你们所知道的一切，你们怎么可能不采取行动呢？

我希望，30年后你们还会再回到哈佛，想起你们用自己的天赋和能力所做出的一切。我希望，在那个时候，你们用来评价自己的标准，不仅仅是你们的专业成就，还包括你们为改变这个世界深刻的不平等所做

who have nothing in common with you but their **humanity**.

　　Good luck.

出的努力,以及你们如何善待那些远隔千山万水、与你们毫无牵涉的人们,你们与他们唯一的共同点就是同为人类。

　　祝各位好运。

单词解析 *Word Analysis*

prevalence ['prevələns] *n.* 流行,盛行;流行程度;普遍,广泛

例 Climate change may also be helping to increase its prevalence.
气候变化可能也会有助于增加其流行程度。

scarcity ['skeəsɪtɪ] *n.* 缺乏;不足

例 This is the world of scarcity.
这是一个资源稀缺的世界。

privileged ['prɪvɪlɪdʒd] *adj.* 有特权的,有特别恩典的

例 She came from a financially privileged background.
她来自经济富足的家庭。

rhetorical [rɪ'tɑrɪkl] *adj.* 修辞学的,修辞的

例 Don't use rhetorical speeches.
别用词藻华丽的台词。

exhort [ɪg'zɔːt] *v.* 规劝;敦促;告诫;激励

例 The teacher exhorted him to work hard.
教师谆谆告诫他要用功。

phenomenal [fɪ'nɑmɪnl] *adj.* 现象的,异常的,能知觉的

例 The rocket travels at phenomenal speed.
火箭以惊人的速度飞行。

barrier ['bærɪə] *n.* 障碍,栅栏

例 The Sahara Desert is a natural barrier between North and Central Africa.
撒哈拉沙漠是北非与中非之间的天然屏障。

awareness [ə'weənəs] *n.* 察觉；体认；觉悟

例 Once you lose awareness, you lose.
一旦你失去了意识，你就完了。

torment [tɔr'ment] *n.* 痛苦；痛苦的根源；苦恼 *v.* 使痛苦，折磨；纠缠；烦扰；作弄

例 Stop tormenting your sister.
别再作弄你姐姐了。

humanity [hjuː'mænətɪ] *n.* 人性；博爱；人类

例 We should treat people and animals with humanity.
我们应该以仁慈之心对待人和动物。

语法知识点 Grammar Points

① Should Harvard encourage its faculty to take on the world's worst inequities?

这个句子中有一个结构"encourage sb. to do sth."，表示"鼓励某人干某事"。

例 Her parents encouraged her to study hard.
她的父母鼓励她好好学习。

② Should Harvard students learn about the depth of global poverty...the prevalence of world hunger...the scarcity of clean water...the girls kept out of school...the children who die from diseases we can cure?

这个句子中有两个结构"learn about..."和"die from..."，分别表示"了解，学习"和"死于……，因……而死"。

例 You can learn about other people.
你可以从中向他人学习。

He died from cancer.
他死于癌症。

③ In line with the promise of this age, I want to exhort each of the graduates here to take on an issue.

这个句子中有两个结构"in line with..."和"take on...",分别表示"符合,和……一致"和"承担;具有;接纳;穿上"。

例 This is because their wages are unlikely to rise in line with the growth in the economy.
这是因为他们的工资不可能以与经济增长保持一致的速度上涨。

As your strength grows, you can take on bigger challenges.
当你的能力增长了,你就可以接受更大的挑战。

④ **You have more than we had; you must start sooner and carry on longer.**

这个句子中有两个结构"more than"和"carry on",分别表示"多于,比……多"和"继续,参与"。前者的反义词是less than,少于。

例 That would be more than I have expected.
那已经比我期望的还要多了。

They will carry on their negotiations next week.
他们将于下周继续进行谈判。

⑤ **And I hope you will come back here to Harvard 30 years from now and reflect on what you have done with your talent and your energy.**

这个句子中有一个结构"reflect on",表示"仔细考虑,思考,反省"。同义词组是reflect upon。

例 We should often reflect on our past mistakes.
我们应当经常反省自己过去的错误。

经典名句 Famous Classics

1. Better keep yourself clean and bright, you are the window through which you must see the world.
   我们透过自身这扇窗观望世界,因此,最好让它保持干净明亮。

2. Towering genius disdains a beaten path. It seeks regions hitherto unexplored. —Lincoln
   卓越的天才不屑走旁人走过的路。他寻找迄今未开拓的地区。(林肯)

3. Learning without thought is labor lost, thought without learning is

perilous. —Confucius
学而不思则罔，思而不学则殆。（孔子）

4. I could be bounded in a nut shell and count myself a king of infinite space.
即使把我关在果壳之中，仍然自以为无限空间之王。

5. There are no ambitions noble enough to justify breaking someone's heart.
没有任何理想会崇高到成为伤一个人心的正当理由。

读书笔记

35 Focus Plus Time Equals Success A
直觉+时间=成功 A

Tim Cook
蒂姆·库克

My most **significant** discovery so far in my life was the result of one single decision: My decision to join Apple. Working at Apple was never in any plan that I'd **outlined** for myself, but was without a doubt the best decision that I ever made. The decision to come to Apple which I made in early 1998 was not so **obvious**.

Apple was in a very different place than it is today, and my employer at the time, Compaq Computer, was the largest personal computer company in the world. Not only was Compaq performing much better than Apple, it was **headquartered** in Texas and therefore closer to Auburn football. Any purely rational consideration of cost and benefits lined up in Compaq's favor, and the people who knew me best advised me to stay at Compaq. One CEO I consulted felt so strongly about it he told me I would be a fool to leave

在我的生命中，我迄今为止最重要的心得体会来源于一个决定：加入苹果。在苹果工作，从来没有被列入我的人生规划中，但是它毫无疑问是我做过的最英明的决定。我1998年早期决定来苹果的决心并不明显。

苹果当年的境遇可谓是步履维艰。而在当时，我所在的公司——康柏电脑是全球最大的个人电脑公司。不仅康柏的业绩比苹果好很多，而且它的总部位于德克萨斯州，离奥本橄榄球队更近。任何理智的人权衡利弊后都会选择康柏，当时我周围的人也建议我留在康柏。我曾经向一位CEO咨询此事，他果断地说，如果我离开康柏而选择苹果，我就是一个傻子。

在决定是否进入苹果时，我必须运用我作为工程师的思

Compaq for Apple.

In making the decision to come to Apple, I had to think beyond my training as an engineer. Engineers are taught to make decisions analytically and largely without emotion. When it comes to a decision between **alternatives**, we **enumerate** the cost and benefits and decide which one is better. But there are times in our lives when the careful consideration of cost and benefits just doesn't seem like the right way to make a decision. There are times in all of our lives when a **reliance** on gut or **intuition** just seems more appropriate-when a particular course of action just feels right. And interestingly I've discovered it's in facing life's most important decisions that intuition seems the most **indispensable** to getting it right.

In turning important decisions over to intuition one has to give up on the idea of developing a life plan that will bear any resemblance to what ultimately unfolds. Intuition is something that occurs in the moment, and if you are open to it, if you listen to it, it has the potential to direct or redirect you in a way that is best for you. On that day in early 1998 I listened to my intuition, not the left side of my brain or for that matter even the people who knew me best. It's hard to know why I listened,

维进行思考。工程师学到的方法就是通过不带任何感情的客观分析来做出决策。当我们面对两个选择的时候，我们就会权衡利弊，选出一个更好的。但是，在我们的生活中，很多时候，精细地权衡利弊似乎并不是做出决定的正确方法。在我们所有人的生活中，有时候依靠直觉做决定似乎更靠谱。有意思的是，我发现在面对人生重大决定的时候，直觉似乎更能让你做出正确的选择。

要把重要的决定权交给直觉，你就必须放弃规划人生未来的想法。直觉决定当下发生的事情。如果你认真聆听它，它就有可能把你导向最适合你的人生道路。在1998年初的那一天，我听从了我的直觉，而不是我的左脑或最了解我的人。我不知道我为什么会这样做，时至今日我也仍然无法确定。但是，在我与史蒂夫·乔布斯会面不到五分钟的时候，我就把逻辑和谨慎抛到了一边，加入了苹果。我的直觉告诉我，加入苹果是一生仅有一次的机会，我能借此机会为富有创意的天才工作，加入可能创造伟大公司的管理团队。如果当时我的直觉在与我左脑斗争的过程中败下阵来，我真不

I'm not even sure I know today, but no more than five minutes into my initial interview with Steve, I wanted to throw caution and logic to the wind and join Apple. My intuition already knew that joining Apple was a once-in-a-lifetime opportunity to work for the creative genius, and to be on the executive team that could **resurrect** a great American company. If my intuition had lost the struggle with my left brain, I'm not sure where I would be today, but I'm certain I would not be standing in front of you.

知道我现在会在哪里，但是肯定不会站在你们面前。

单词解析 Word Analysis

significant [sɪɡˈnɪfɪkənt] *adj.* 重要的，暗示的，有含义的

例 Their change of plan is strange but I don't think it's significant.
他们改变了计划十分奇怪，我觉得没有什么意义。

outline [ˈaʊtlaɪn] *n.* 外形；略图；轮廓；素描 *v.* 描画轮廓，描述要点

例 We outlined our main objections to the proposal.
我们扼要地说明了反对该建议的意见。

obvious [ˈɒbvɪəs] *adj.* 明显的，显然的，明白的

例 It was obvious to everyone that the child had been badly treated.
大家都清楚那孩子受过虐待。

headquarter [ˈhedkwɔːtə] *v.* 以……作总部；设总公司于……

例 The new company will headquarter in Paris.
新公司会将总部设在巴黎。

alternative [ɔːlˈtɜːnətɪv] *n.* 选择，二择一 *adj.* 两者择一的；替代的

例 Have you got an alternative suggestion?
你有没有其他建议？

enumerate [ɪ'njuːməreɪt] *v.* 列举，枚举，计算

> 例 She enumerated the items we had to buy sugar, tea, soap, etc.
> 她列出了我们要购买的东西——糖、茶叶、肥皂等。

reliance [rɪ'laɪəns] *n.* 信任，信赖的人或事，信赖

> 例 Don't place too much reliance on his advice.
> 别太相信他的意见。

intuition [ɪntuː'ɪʃn] *n.* 直觉；直觉的知识

> 例 My intuitions proved correct.
> 我的直觉确实是正确的。

indispensable [ɪndɪ'spensəbl] *adj.* 不可缺少的，绝对必要的，不能避免的

> 例 A good dictionary is indispensable for learning a foreign language.
> 学习外语离不开好的词典。

resurrect [rezə'rekt] *v.* 使复活；使再活跃；使复苏；使再流行；复活

> 例 That noise is enough to resurrect the dead!
> 那噪声都能把死人吵活！

语法知识点 *Grammar Points*

① **Working at Apple was never in any plan that I'd outlined for myself, but was without a doubt the best decision that I ever made.**

这个句子中有一个结构"without a doubt"，表示"毫无疑问"。本句话开头working at Apple是动名词做主语。

> 例 He doesn't love her at all without a doubt.
> 毫无疑问，他根本不爱她。

② **Not only was Compaq performing much better than Apple, it was headquartered in Texas and therefore closer to Auburn football.**

这个句子中有一个结构"be headquartered in some place"，表示"在……设立总部"。

> 例 The new company will be headquartered in Paris.

新公司会将总部设在巴黎。

③ **Any purely rational consideration of cost and benefits lined up in Compaq's favor, and the people who knew me best advised me to stay at Compaq.**

这个句子中有两个结构"in one's favor"和"advise sb. to do sth.",分别表示"支持,偏向某人"和"建议某人干某事"。后者advise也可以直接加that从句,后面要用(should)+动词原形的虚拟语气。

例 I advise that he should leave immediately.
我建议他应该马上离开。

④ **In turning important decisions over to intuition one has to give up on the idea of developing a life plan that will bear any resemblance to what ultimately unfolds.**

这个句子中有一个结构"bear a resemblance to...",表示"与……相似,相像"。Bear可以换成show或者have。

例 Alice shows a great resemblance to her mom.
爱丽丝和她母亲很像。

⑤ **My intuition already knew that joining Apple was a once-in-a-lifetime opportunity to work for the creative genius, and to be on the executive team that could resurrect a great American company.**

这个句子中有一个结构"a once-in-a-lifetime opportunity",表示"千载难逢的机会"。另外在一个团队中用介词on,例如on a football team。

经典名句 Famous Classics

1. Life is always so we covered all over with cuts and bruises, but later, the injured area will become the strong place.
   生活总是让我们遍体鳞伤,但到后来,那些受伤的地方一定会变成我们最强壮的地方。

2. It will never rain roses. When we want to have more roses, we must plant more trees. — George Eliot
   天空可不会下玫瑰雨。想要更多的玫瑰花,我们就得栽下更多的树。
   (乔治·艾略特)

3. I like the dreams of the future better than history of the past!
   对于回忆过去，我更喜欢憧憬未来！

4. Energy and persistence conquer all things.
   能量加毅力可以征服一切。

5. Do anything rather than marry without affection.
   没有爱情万不可成婚。

读书笔记

36 Focus Plus Time Equals Success B
直觉+时间=成功 B

Tim Cook
蒂姆·库克

This was a surprising lesson. I **recall** how uncertain I was at my own commencement about where my life would lead. There was a part of me that very much wanted to have a 25-year plan as a guide to life. When I went to business school we even had an exercise to do a 25-year plan. I found mine, now 22 years old, in preparing for this **commencement** address. Let's just say it wasn't worth the yellowed paper it was written on. I didn't understand it then as a young MBA student, but life has a habit of throwing you curve balls. Don't get me wrong-it's good to plan for the future, but if you're like me and you **occasionally** want to swing for the fences, you can't count on a **predictable** life. But even if you can't plan, you can prepare. A great batter doesn't know when the high-hanging curve ball is going to come, but he knows it will.

这是一个深刻的教训。我还记得，在我毕业的时候，我也感到茫然，不知道我的生活将会通往何方。我很想设定一个25年的规划来引领我的人生。当我念商学院的时候，我们甚至练习做一个25年的人生规划。现在22年过去了，我已在为你们的毕业典礼准备演讲稿了。当我还是一个年轻的MBA学生时，我并不明白，生活经常会向你投来曲线球。别误会我——我并不是说人生不需要规划。规划人生未来没有错，但是如果你像我一样，偶尔想去看看篱笆外面的风景，你就不要指望按部就班的生活。但是，即使你不规划人生，你也能着手准备。伟大的棒球手并不知道曲线球什么时候飞过来，但是他知道它会飞过来。于是，他就开始准备，

And he can prepare for what he will do when he gets it.

Too often people think about intuition as the same as relying on luck or faith. At least as I see it, nothing could be further from the truth. Intuition can tell you that of the doors that are open to you, which one you should walk through. But intuition cannot prepare you for what's on the other side of that door. Along these lines a quote that has always **resonated** with me is one by Abraham Lincoln. He said "I will prepare, and some day my chance will come." I have always believed this. It was this basic belief that led me to Auburn to study industrial engineering, led me to co-op alternating quarters while **attending** Auburn, led me to Duke to study business, and led me to accept so many jobs and assignments that are too **numerous** to mention.

等待时机给它用力一击。

人们经常把直觉等同于运气或信念。至少在我看来，直觉距离真理最近。直觉能告诉你哪扇门是对你开放的，你应该从这扇门里走出去。但是，直觉不能让你准备好迎接门外面的东西。我经常想起亚伯拉罕·林肯说过的一句话："我将会认真准备，直到机会有一天到来。"我深信不疑。正是这种信仰引领我到奥本大学学习工业工程，引领我到杜克大学学习商业，引领我接受了难以计数的工作和任务。

单词解析 *Word Analysis*

recall [rɪˈkɔl] *n.* 回想，回忆；叫回 *v.* 回想，回忆；召回

例　I can't recall his name.
　　我想不起他的名字了。

commencement [kəˈmensm(ə)nt] *n.* 开始，毕业典礼

例　The commencement was held in the grand hall.
　　毕业典礼在豪华的大厅举行。

occasionally [əˈkeɪʒnəlɪ] *adv.* 偶尔，间或

例 Disputes occasionally occurred between us.
我们之间偶尔也会有一番争论。

predictable [prɪˈdɪktəbl] *adj.* 可预言的

例 Traditional development is not predictable.
传统的开发是不可预言的。

resonate [ˈrezəneɪt] *v.* 共鸣；共振；起回声

例 That statement doesn't resonate with many people.
那些声明与许多人没有共鸣。

attend [əˈtend] *v.* 参加；出席；照顾

例 They had a quiet wedding: only a few friends attended (it).
他们的婚礼静悄悄的——只有几个朋友参加。

numerous [ˈnuːmərəs] *adj.* 很多的，多数的，数目众多的

例 I have numerous engagements next week.
下星期我有许多约会。

语法知识点 *Grammar Points*

① ...but if you're like me and you occasionally want to swing for the fences, you can't count on a predictable life.

这个句子中有一个结构"count on..."，表示"依赖，指望，依靠"。同义词组是rely on和depend on，on可以换成upon。Be like的意思是像……，like在这里是介词。

例 Don't count on me.
别指望我。

② But even if you can't plan, you can prepare.

这个句子中有一个结构"even if"，表示"即使，虽然"，同义词组是even though。

例 Even if it rains tomorrow, we will continue our work.
即使明天下雨，我们也要继续工作。

Focus Plus Time Equals Success B
直觉+时间=成功 B

③ It was this basic belief that led me to Auburn to study industrial engineering, led me to co-op alternating quarters while attending Auburn, led me to Duke to study business, and led me to accept so many jobs and assignments that are too numerous to mention.

这个句子中有三个结构 "lead sb. to sp.", "lead sb. to do sth." 和 "too...to...", 分别表示 "带领某人去某处", 这里的to是介词; "带领某人干某事", 这里的to是动词不定式; 以及 "太……而不能"。

例 She led me to the school and led me to learn English but I was too young to follow.
她带领我去了学校，带着我学习英语，但是我太小跟不上。

经典名句 Famous Classics

1. The greatest use of life is to spend it for something that will outlast it.
   将生命花在比生命更长久的事上，就是尽用生命。

2. The human race has one really effective weapon, and that is laughter.
   人类拥有一强而有力的武器，叫作欢笑。

3. People die, but books never die. No man and no force can abolish memory.
   人会死亡，书却无朽。没有任何人可以丢弃记忆。

4. Never let fear or shame keep you from celebrating the unique people that you are.
   绝不要让害怕或羞怯，阻止你欣赏自己的独一无二。

5. The best and most beautiful things in the world cannot be seen or even touched. They must be felt with the heart.
   世上最美好的事物看不着也摸不到，它们只能用心感觉。

37 Focus Plus Time Equals Success C
直觉+时间=成功 C

Tim Cook
蒂姆·库克

In business as in sports, the **vast** majority of victories are determined before the beginning of the game. We **rarely** control the timing of opportunities, but we can control our preparation. I feel Lincoln's quote is especially appropriate now, given the state of the economy and the worry that I **suspect** a number of you must feel. I had the same worry when I graduated in 1982 (yes, I am prehistoric, for the record). But as many of the parents here will remember, the economy then bore some strong similarities to the economy today. The unemployment rate was in the double digits, we didn't have the collapse of Wall Street banks but we did have the savings and loan **crisis**. I worried, as many of my classmates did, what the future held for them.

But what was true for Lincoln was true for those of us who graduated

商场如赛场，绝大多数成功在比赛开始之前就已经决定了。我们不能控制机会来临的时间，但是我们能够控制我们的准备工作。就目前的经济形势以及我们时常感受到的担心而言，林肯的话在今天尤其适用。当我在1982年毕业的时候，我也有着和你们一样的担心。在座的很多学生家长可能还记得，当时的经济状态与现在实际上差不了多少。失业率高达两位数字，尽管没有华尔街银行倒闭，但是我们有着严重的储蓄和信贷危机。和我的很多同班同学一样，我也很担心自己的未来。

但是，适用于林肯的至理名言也同样适用于我们82届毕业的学生，当然也同样适用于今天毕业的你们。机会垂青有准备的头脑。就像所有的前

in '82, and it is true for those of you graduating today. Prepare and your chance will come. Just as all **previous** generations have done you will stand on the shoulders of the generation that came before you. The generation of mine and your parents. And you will **achieve** more and go farther. The fact that you are here now at this great institution, in this great state, at this great moment for both you and your families is a testament to the fact that your preparation has begun. Continue to prepare yourselves as you have at Auburn, so when your gut tells you "this is my moment," you are without a doubt ready.

If you are prepared, when the right door opens then it comes down to just one more thing: Make sure that your execution lives up to your preparation. At least for me the second sentence of the Auburn creed, "I believe in work, hard work" really resonates here and has been one of my core beliefs for as long as I can remember. Though the sentiment is a simple one, there's **tremendous** dignity and wisdom in these words, and they have stood the test of time.

As current events teach us, those who try to achieve success without hard work ultimately **deceive** themselves, or worse, deceive others. I have the good fortune to be surrounded by some

辈人一样，你们将会站在你们上一代人的肩膀上，也就是我和你们的父母这一代人的肩膀上。你们将会看得更远，取得更大的成就。在这个伟大的时刻，你们和你们的家人汇聚在这个伟大的学校，这证明你们的准备已经开始了。毕业后，你们还要像你们在奥本大学所做的那样，继续用知识武装你们自己。只有这样，当你的直觉告诉你"我的机会来临"时，你就能信心百倍地准备迎接它了。

当你已准备好，而且正确的大门也已向你敞开，你就只需要做一件事了：行动起来。至少对我而言，奥本大学校训中的第二句话"我相信工作，艰苦地工作"能让我产生很大的共鸣，而且一直是我的核心信念之一。这是一句很朴实的话，但却蕴含着无穷的智慧和尊严。而且，它们也经受住了时间的检验。

无数事例告诉我们，那些想要不费吹灰之力就取得成功的人终究是在欺骗他们自己，甚至是在欺骗别人。我非常幸运，我的周围有很多睿智的、听从直觉的思想家，他们创造了全世界最精致、最杰出的产品。对于我们来说，直觉

brilliant, intuitive thinkers who create the most elegant and extraordinary products in the world. For all of us intuition is not a substitute for **rigorous** thinking and hard work: It is simply the lead-in. We never take shortcuts. We attend to every detail. We follow where curiosity leads, aware that the journey may be longer but will ultimately be more **worthwhile**. We take risks knowing that risk will sometimes result in failure. But without the possibility of failure, there is no possibility of success. We remember Albert Einstein's words: "Insanity is doing the same things over and over again and expecting different results." When you put it all together, I know this: Intuition is critical in virtually everything you do, but without relentless preparation and execution, it is meaningless.

不能取代缜密的思维和艰苦的工作，它只能把我们引进门，修行还得靠个人。我们没有捷径可走。我们必须关注每一个细节，听从好奇心的指引。我们清楚，整个过程可能非常漫长，但是最终它是值得的。我们敢于冒险，也知道冒险有时候会导致失败。但是，没有失败，又何谈成功？我们牢记阿尔伯特·爱因斯坦的话："疯狂就是反复做同一件事情，并期待有不一样的结果。"总而言之，直觉对你做的任何事情都很重要。但是，如果没有坚持不懈的准备和行动，它就会变得毫无意义。

单词解析 Word Analysis

vast [vɑːst] *adj.* 巨大的，非常的，广大的

例 His business empire was truly vast.
他的企业规模极大。

rarely ['reəlɪ] *adv.* 很少，难得；出色地；异乎寻常地

例 He rarely mingles with other students on the campus.
他很少和校园里的其他学生交往。

suspect [sə'spekt] *n.* 嫌疑犯；可疑分子 *v.* 疑有，察觉；怀疑；不信任 *adj.* 令人怀疑的，可疑的

例 He suspected an ambush.
他感到有埋伏。

crisis ['kraɪsɪs] *n.* 危机，紧要关头，危险期
例 In times of crisis, it's good to have a friend to turn to.
危难时好在有朋友可以投奔。

previous ['priːvɪəs] *adj.* 早先的，过急的，前面的
例 We had met on a previous occasion.
我们上次见过面。

achieve [ə'tʃiːv] *v.* 实现，完成；赢得，达到
例 I've achieved only half of what I'd hoped to do.
我希望做到的，我仅完成了一半。

tremendous [trɪ'mendəs] *adj.* 巨大的，可怕的，非常的
例 It makes a tremendous difference to me.
这对我来说差别极大。

deceive [dɪ'siːv] *v.* 欺骗，蒙蔽；哄骗做；欺诈，行骗
例 We were deceived into believing that he could help us.
我们受骗了，还以为他能帮助我们。

rigorous ['rɪɡərəs] *adj.* 严格的；苛刻的；严厉的；严酷的
例 Our teacher is so rigorous that he seldom lets up on us.
我们的老师很严格，他很少放松对我们的要求。

worthwhile [wɜː'θwaɪl] *adj.* 值得做的，值得花时间的
例 The trip is not worthwhile.
跑这一趟不值。

语法知识点 *Grammar Points*

① **In business as in sports, the vast majority of victories are determined before the beginning of the game.**

这个句子中有一个结构"the vast majority of..."，表示"大多数……"，相当于most。

例 The vast majority of students were here.
大多数学生都在这里。

② **I feel Lincoln's quote is especially appropriate now, given the state of the economy and the worry that I suspect a number of you must feel.**

这个句子中有一个结构"given..."，表示"考虑到（某事物）"，given后面可以加名词词组也可以加that从句。这个句子里还有一个that引导的定语从句，...the worry that I suspect a number of you must feel，表示我猜想你们很多人感受到的担心。

例 Given her interest in children/ Given that she is interested in children, I am sure teaching is the right career for her.
考虑到她喜欢孩子，我可以肯定教书是最适合她的职业。

③ **But what was true for Lincoln was true for those of us who graduated in '82, and it is true for those of you graduating today.**

这个句子中有一个结构"be true for..."，表示"对……适用，符合于……"。

例 This is especially true for old people.
这对老年人尤其适用。

④ **Make sure that your execution lives up to your preparation.**

这个句子中有两个结构"make sure"和"live up to"，分别表示"确保"和"不辜负"。Make sure后面可以加that从句，也可以加of（doing）sth.。

例 So make sure you do things on time.
所以一定要按时做该做的事情。
Our children try to live up to our expectations.
我们的孩子努力不辜负我们的期望。

⑤ **We attend to every detail.**

这个句子中"attend to"表示"照料，注意，致力于"，相当于take care of。

例 I must attend to my feet.
我必须爱护自己的脚。

经典名句 *Famous Classics*

1. It is better to live your own destiny imperfectly than to live an imitation of somebody else's life with perfection.
   不完美地走自己的命运比完美地模仿别人的生活还要好。

2. The art of being happy lies in the power of extracting happiness from common things.
   快乐的艺术在于由平凡提取快乐的能力。

3. Action is the real measure of intelligence.
   行动是智慧的真正衡量标准。

4. In your pursuit of your passions, always be young. In your relationship with others, always be grown-up.
   追求兴趣时保持年轻，与人相处时保持成熟。

5. There are many more people trying to meet the right person than to become the right person.
   很多人想遇到对的人，而不是让自己成为对的人。

读书笔记

我的演讲美文：神奇的时代

读书笔记